THE ART OF
MANLINESS

THE ART OF
MANLINESS

Classic Skills and Manners
for the Modern Man

Brett and Kate McKay

HOW BOOKS

Cincinnati, Ohio
www.howdesign.com

For more excellent books and resources for designers, visit www.howdesign.com.

15 14 13 12 11   10 9 8 7

Distributed in Canada by Fraser Direct, 100 Armstrong Avenue, Georgetown, Ontario, Canada L7G 5S4, Tel: (905) 877-4411. Distributed in the U.K. and Europe by David & Charles, Brunel House, Newton Abbot, Devon, TQ12 4PU, England, Tel: (+44) 1626 323200, Fax: (+44) 1626 323319, E-mail: postmaster@ davidandcharles.co.uk. Distributed in Australia by Capricorn Link, P.O. Box 704, Windsor, NSW 2756 Australia, Tel: (02) 4577-3555.

Library of Congress Cataloging-in-Publication Data

McKay, Brett.
  The art of manliness : classic skills and manners for the modern man / by Brett and Kate McKay.
      p. cm.
  Includes index.
  ISBN 978-1-60061-462-0 (pbk. : alk. paper)
  1. Men--Identity. 2. Masculinity. 3. Sex role. I. McKay, Kate. II. Title.
  HQ1090.M396 2009
  155.3'32--dc22

                                                                    2009008753

Edited by Amy Schell
Designed by Grace Ring
Illustrated by Josh Roflow
Cover illustration © 2009 Jupiterimages
Production coordinated by Greg Nock

ABOUT THE AUTHORS

Brett McKay is a man. Kate McKay loves manly men.
Together this husband and wife team reside
in Tulsa, Oklahoma, and run the ArtofManliness.com,
the manliest website on the Internet.

DEDICATION

To William Hurst and George Novak,
members of the Greatest Generation
and men who truly lived the art of manliness.

WILLIAM HURST

GEORGE NOVAK

"It is not the critic who counts; not the man who points out how the strong man stumbles, or where the doer of deeds could have done them better. The credit belongs to the man who is actually in the arena, whose face is marred by dust and sweat and blood; who strives valiantly; who errs, who comes short again and again, because there is no effort without error and shortcoming; but who does actually strive to do the deeds; who knows great enthusiasms, the great devotions; who spends himself in a worthy cause; who at the best knows in the end the triumph of high achievement, and who at the worst, if he fails, at least fails while daring greatly, so that his place shall never be with those cold and timid souls who neither know victory nor defeat."

—THEODORE ROOSEVELT

CONTENTS

INTRODUCTION

"He is going to be known as a sort of boys' hero.
He is going to be known preeminently for his manliness.
There is going to be a Roosevelt legend."

———•———

"I have grieved most deeply at the death of your noble son.
I have watched his conduct from the commencement of the war,
and have pointed with pride to the patriotism, self-denial,
and manliness of character he has exhibited."

———•———

"After all, the greatest of Washington's qualities
was a rugged manliness which gave him the respect and
confidence even of his enemies."

The quotes above are taken from nineteenth-century writings, and show the use of the word manliness in a way quite foreign to the modern reader: as a great compliment. In times past, manliness was a worthy and distinct characteristic, like intelligence, bravery and humor. It was a quality that boys strived to attain and men wished to have attached to their name.

A man who had mastered the art of manliness embodied many, if not all, of these manly characteristics:

- Looks out for and is loyal to his friends and family.
- Does the right thing, even when it's not convenient.

- Is proficient in the manly arts.
- Treats women with respect and honor.
- Serves and gives back to his community.
- Sacrifices for the good of others.
- Works hard and seldom complains.
- Exhibits both great courage and tender compassion.
- Has a confident swagger but isn't a pompous jerk.
- Is witty without succumbing to sarcasm.
- Embraces instead of shirks responsibility.

You probably have grandfathers who exemplify this kind of honorable manliness. But something happened in the last fifty years to cause these positive manly virtues and skills to disappear from the current generations of men. Fathers have ceased passing on the art of manliness to their sons, and our culture, nervous to assign any single set of virtues to one sex, has stripped the meaning of manliness of anything laudatory.

Discouraged from celebrating the positive aspects of manliness, society today focuses only on the stereotypical and negative aspects of manhood. Sadly manliness has come to be associated with the dithering dads of televisions sitcoms and commercials, the shallow action dudes of cinema who live to blow stuff up and the meatheads of men's magazines who covet six-pack abs above all else.

Our goal with this book is to hopefully encourage a new generation of men to pick up where their grandfathers left off in the history and legacy of manliness. Many people have argued that we need to reinvent what manliness means in the twenty-first century. Usually this means stripping manliness of its masculinity and replacing it with more sensitive feminine qualities. We argue that manliness doesn't need to be reinvented.

The art of manliness just needs to be rediscovered.

While no book could ever fully cover all the positive qualities and essential skills every man should possess, we hope this book can at least get men started down the path of rediscovering the lost art of manliness. We've divided the book into several sections reflecting the different roles a man assumes throughout his life. Within each section we discuss a sampling of the attributes and skills that many men today have never learned. You can read the book straight through or you can skip to parts that you find more interesting or pertinent to your own life.

Don't let this book be the end of your journey to rediscover the lost art of manliness; it should only be the beginning. Thousands of men before us have left behind nuggets of wisdom that describe what it means to be a man. And if you look hard enough, you can find men in your own life who can teach you the important skills and qualities of true manhood. Seek out great men, both past and present, and in time you'll become a virtuoso of the art of manliness.

NOTE TO READERS: Not only have many of the skills of the men of yesteryear been lost over time, so has a great deal of the colorful language that was once spoken in the streets and saloons of nineteenth-century cities. We've given the pages of this book a SMART SPRINKLE (a good deal) of these old-time phrases and expressions. (They are indicated by SMALL CAPS throughout the book.) So if you come across a word that sounds like something your great-great-great grandpa might have said, it probably is. On page 271 (Appendix B) you'll find a glossary with these nineteenth-century slang words and their definitions.

Also, because the oft-used "douche bag" is getting as old as "bling bling," we've peppered the pages of this book with unique insults from our manliest president, Theodore Roosevelt. TR was master of the creative, yet cutting, put-down. These are also denoted by SMALL CAPS. To freshen up your insult repertoire, turn to page 274 for a full list of TR's humdingers. This page can be cut out and carried in your wallet for an easy reference the next time you catch your coworker stealing your lunch from the office fridge.

CHAPTER ONE

✦|THE|✦
GENTLEMAN

"This is the final test of a gentleman: his respect
for those who can be of no possible service to him."
—WILLIAM LYON PHELPS

For centuries, well-bred men were trained in all the manly arts, from the skills needed to be a soldier to the proper etiquette for dinner parties. They were quintessential gentlemen–dapper in dress, polite in conduct, yet every bit a true man. Unfortunately, many modern men place the gentleman on the sissy end of the manliness spectrum, opposite that of the burping, unshaven, uncouth, "man's man." Yet our forebears understood that there was no contradiction in being ruggedly manly and a refined gentleman. George Washington, Theodore Roosevelt and Robert E. Lee are some examples of men who combined gritty manliness with gentlemanly bearing. They paid attention to how they dressed, groomed and conducted themselves and were as comfortable at a stately ball as they were on the battlefield. And the desire to be a gentleman was not restricted to the rich or powerful either; Emily Post's *Etiquette* was the most requested book by G.I.s during World War II.

Unfortunately, not enough men today have taken the time to cultivate both the hearty and the refined sides of their manly character. It sometimes seems the gentleman is a dying breed. Common decency and respectful etiquette have been replaced with unrepentant rudeness. Today's men walk around ungroomed in wrinkled and ill-fitted clothing and often have little regard for how their behavior affects others.

But it doesn't have to be this way.

Being a gentleman is more than following a bunch of dos and don'ts. It's about having a profound respect for yourself and for others. By following the simple tips contained in this chapter, any ruffian can turn into a proper gentleman. Developing the traits of a gentleman is a key to success in all aspects of your life. Business associates will respect you; friends will flock to you; women will adore you.

"The difference between a man of sense and a fop is that the fop values himself upon his dress; and the man of sense laughs at it, at the same time he knows he must not neglect it."

—LORD CHESTERFIELD

Judging a book by its cover may not be desirable, but it's initially the only evidence we have at our disposal. Within seconds of meeting you, people make judgments and decisions based on your appearance. What are your clothes telling them? That you're a disciplined, thoughtful guy with an eye for detail? Or that you're just sliding by in life?

Appearance matters. Dressing like a gentleman will boost your own confidence and win you the respect of others. Whether you're applying for a job or taking a lady out on the town, putting your best foot forward will maximize your chances for success. Especially if that foot is covered by a well-shined shoe.

Getting Fitted for a Suit

"Like every good man, I strive for perfection, and, like every ordinary man, I have found that perfection is out of reach—but not the perfect suit."

—EDWARD TIVNAN

There's no manlier outfit than a well tailored suit. The reason they look so darn manly is that they originated from military uniforms. Every man should have at least one good suit that he can wear to job interviews, weddings and a special night on the town. But picking out a suit is not like picking out a T-shirt and a pair of jeans. If you want to look and feel good in your suit, you need to take into account several factors. Below, we've provided some things to keep in mind when you walk into a haberdashery to get fitted for a new suit. Follow them, and you'll leave the store with a long-lasting and dashingly handsome suit.

The Jacket: Getting the Perfect Fit

Fit the shoulder. The most important area you want to check for fit is in the shoulder or yoke area of the jacket. While you can alter a suit that doesn't fit in the shoulder, it's much more difficult than other areas of the jacket and will thus cost more. You don't want the fabric in the shoulder to be so tight that it starts to bunch up. The shoulder and upper back area should lie flat along your body.

Make sure the armholes are comfortable. When you lay your arms down at your side, it shouldn't feel like the armholes are digging their way into your armpits. If you can't put your arms down, you definitely have a problem. You don't want to be Randy in *A Christmas Story*, looking like a tick ready to pop. Again, while the armholes can be altered, it's much more difficult and will cost you a lot of money. **(FIGURE 1.1)**

Check how the jacket drapes on your body. The suit should drape comfortably and freely on the front of your body. It shouldn't drape so much that you look like a twelve-year-old borrowing your dad's suit. The lapels should lay flat on your chest. If they're not, it's too small. Finally, check the back. If the jacket has vents, then the vents should lay flat on your butt, i.e., your butt shouldn't be sticking out. If it is, you need to have the jacket altered so it fits larger around your front.

Check the length of the jacket. The key here is to find balance. You

FIGURE 1.1 The most important area you want to check for fit is in the shoulder or yoke area of the jacket.

don't want the jacket to be too long or too short. Your grandpa's tailor used to check for the proper length of the jacket by having him lay his arms at his side and cup his fingers. The jacket was fitted to where it met the inner curve of Grandpa's fingers. The modern rule of thumb is that the jacket should be long enough to completely cover your butt, but no longer.

Check the length of the sleeve. Sleeves should generally be long enough to show just a quarter length of shirtsleeve when you lay your arms flat at your side. You don't want the sleeve to break past your wrist. That's nerdy.

Pants: Where Should the Trouser Break?

Wear your pants on your waist, not your hips. We're talking about your real waist here. For the past twenty years men have been wearing their pants lower and lower around their hips. While this may be fine for jeans, wearing your pants very low does not work for trousers. A man should wear trousers at navel level, not below it.

When your tailor is talking about "the break in your trouser," he's talking about the point where your pant's hem falls on your shoes. If your break is too high, you'll look like Steve Urkel. If it's too low, your pants will swallow your DEW BEATERS. You have three options for where the break is on your pant: the full break, the medium break and the no break. **(FIGURE 1.2)**

The full break: The bottom of the hem covers the heel of the shoe. This option provides a much longer covering, keeping the pants from exposing one's socks when walking.

The medium break: The bottom of the hem falls in the middle of the heel of the shoe. It provides less covering for the sock when walking but keeps the fabric further away from the floor and reduces the chance of tripping.

The no break: The bottom of the hem falls almost at the top of the heel of the shoe. When being measured for a no break hem, make sure the tailor doesn't go too high or you'll show too much sock.

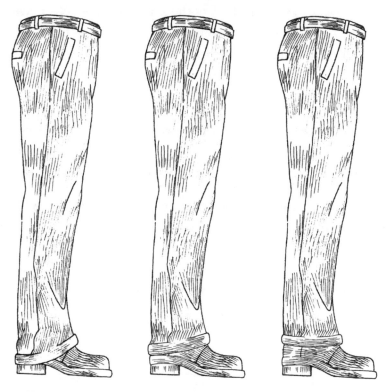

FIGURE 1.2 You have three options for where the break is on your pant. From left to right: the full break, the medium break and the no break.

HOW TO ROCK A POCKET SQUARE

What do Winston Churchill, Cary Grant, and James Bond have in common? In addition to enjoying a stiff drink, they all rocked a pocket square. Like the hat, the popularity of pocket squares waxes and wanes, and for too long men were neglecting the breast pockets of their suits.

But the pocket square is currently enjoying a renaissance, popping up on the movers and shakers in Hollywood and hip hop. Hell, even

Saddam Hussein rocked a pocket square when he was on trial—a man should never defend his war crimes without one.

The pocket square is back with good reason; they are an easy and inexpensive way to vary the look of the same suit. Pocket squares add some visual interest and flair to your appearance. Every man just looks more dapper with a bit of fabric peeking out his pocket.

Pocket Square Guidelines

Don't leave your suit naked. A suit without a pocket square lacks finished panache. So the first guideline of pocket square usage is to always wear one when you wear a suit or sport coat. It just looks better.

Color coordinating. A pocket square can be patterned or solid. The general guideline is that your pocket square color should complement some color on your tie. So if your tie has a bit of red, rock a solid red pocket square or a patterned pocket square with some red in it. However, avoid matching the colors exactly. It looks like you're trying too hard (so never ever buy a tie/pocket square set at your local department store). A white pocket square can be worn with any color tie, making the white handkerchief an essential part of every man's collection.

How to Fold a Pocket Square

You have several options on how to fold your pocket square. Some are quite simple and others are complex. It all comes down to personal taste. Here are three simple folds that every man should master. **(FIGURE 1.3)**

THE STRAIGHT FOLD
The straight fold lends a classic look to your suit. What you'll end up with is a small rectangle peeking out of your breast pocket. Here's one way to fold it:

1. Lay your pocket square flat.
2. Bring the left side to the right side
3. Bring the bottom towards the top, but don't fold it all the way.
4. Fold the fabric in thirds horizontally so that it will fit your suit pocket.

THE ONE CORNER FOLD

With the one corner fold, you'll have a small peak of fabric coming out your pocket. This one is my favorite of the three. Here's how to fold it:

1. Lay your pocket square on a flat surface with one corner facing up and one corner facing down so it looks like you have a baseball diamond in front of you.
2. Bring the bottom point to the top point so that you create a triangle.
3. Bring the left corner of the triangle to the right corner, and the right corner to the left corner. You should end up with a long rectangle with a point at the top. It looks sort of like a fence slat.

FIGURE 1.3 Here are three simple folds that every man should master. From left to right: the straight fold, the one corner fold and the puff fold.

4. Fold the bottom toward the top, but not all the way.

5. Place it in your suit. Adjust until you get the desired amount of point coming out of the pocket.

THE PUFF FOLD

The puff "fold" is the simplest of the folds, as there's no actual folding involved. The result is a small puff of fabric coming out of your suit pocket. Here's how to do it.

1. Lay the pocket square flat.

2. Pinch the middle of the fabric, allowing the folds to come in naturally.

3. With one hand firmly holding the pocket square, use your other hand to gently gather it together.

4. Now gracefully gather up the bottom of the pocket square.

5. Place it in your suit. Fiddle with it until you get the desired puffiness.

THREE WAYS TO TIE A TIE

It's a sad fact, but there are grown men who don't know how to tie a necktie. If they have a big interview that afternoon, they'll go shopping for a clip-on. Even if a man does know how to tie a tie, their knowledge is often limited to just one knot. But there are several ways to tie a necktie. Certain knots should be used with certain shirt collars and tie fabric materials to get the best results for your appearance. Below, we show you three classic necktie knots every man should know and give you the lowdown on when you should use them. (FIGURE 1.4)

THE WINDSOR KNOT

The Windsor knot gives you a wide triangular knot that's good for more formal settings. This knot is best worn with a wide spread collar.

FIGURE 1.4 Here are three classic necktie knots every man should know. From left to right: the Windsor knot, the half Windsor knot and the four-in-hand knot.

1. Drape the tie around your neck. The wide end should extend about 12 inches below the narrow end of the tie. Cross the wide part of the tie over the narrow end.
2. Bring the wide end of the tie up through the hole between your collar and the tie. Then pull it down toward the front.
3. Bring the wide end behind the narrow end and to the right.
4. Pull the wide end back through the loop again. You should have a triangle now where the knot will be.
5. Wrap the wide end around the triangle by pulling the wide end from right to left.
6. Bring the wide end up through the loop a third time.
7. Pull the wide end through the knot in front.
8. Tighten the knot and center it with both hands.

THE HALF WINDSOR KNOT

This is the Windsor knot's little brother. Like the Windsor, you're left with a symmetrical triangle knot, but the Half Windsor is not as large. This knot is appropriate for lighter fabrics and wider ties. It's best worn with a standard collar.

1. Drape the tie around your neck. The wide end should extend about 12 inches below the narrow end of the tie. Cross the wide part of the tie over the narrow end.
2. Bring the wide end around and behind the narrow end.
3. Bring the wide end up and pull it down through the hole between your collar and tie.
4. Bring the wide end around the front, over the narrow end from right to left.
5. Bring the wide end up back through the loop again.
6. Pull the wide end down through the knot in front.
7. Tighten the knot and center it with both hands.

THE FOUR-IN-HAND KNOT

Also known as the "schoolboy," this is probably the most widely used knot because it's so easy to tie. It's a good knot to use if your tie is made of heavier material. It looks best with smaller spread collars.

1. Drape the tie around your neck. The wide end should extend about 12 inches below the narrow end of the tie. Cross the wide part of the tie over the narrow end.
2. Turn the wide end back underneath the narrow end.
3. Continue wrapping the wide end around the narrow end by bringing it across the front of the narrow end again.
4. Pull the wide end up and through the back of the loop.
5. Hold the front of the knot with your index finger and bring the wide end down through the front knot.
6. Tighten the knot carefully to the GILLS by holding the narrow end and sliding the knot up. Center the knot.

BRINGING BACK THE HAT

And now for the ultimate finishing touch for any gentleman's outfit: the hat.

Up until the 1950s, men were rarely seen out and about without a hat sitting upon their heads. Since that time, the wearing of hats has seen a precipitous decline. No one is sure why. Some say the downfall of hats occurred when JFK did not wear a hat to his inauguration, thus forever branding them as uncool. This is an urban myth, however, as Kennedy did indeed don a hat that day. Another theory posits that the shrinking size of cars made wearing a hat while driving prohibitively difficult. Most likely, the demise of hats can simply be traced to changing styles and the ongoing trend toward a more casual look.

Yet hats are due for a full resurgence. Hats are both functional and stylish. They can hide a bad hair day, cover a bald spot, keep your head warm and shade your eyes from the sun. Hats supply a touch of class and sophistication, impart personality and add an interesting and unique accent to your outfits. And hats are a surefire way to boost your confidence. A cool hat can quickly become your signature piece and give you extra swagger.

The Different Kinds of Hats

Of course men today still wear hats, but they are most often confined to ratty baseball caps, hippie beanie caps or the thankfully almost extinct trucker hat. There is nothing wrong with these kinds of headpieces per se, but there are other hat options out there. So mix up your lids with the following options.

THE FLAT CAP
The flat cap has a rounded shape, a small brim and a high back. Long associated with working-class men in the UK, the flat cap can be a stylish way to add interest to a casual outfit. They can give your tired jeans and T-shirt look unique style. Choose the more masculine flat cap over the similar, but rounder and puffier, newsboy cap. The latter has been almost entirely co-opted by the ladies. **(FIGURE 1.5)**

FIGURE 1.5 The flat cap.

FIGURE 1.6 The fedora.

FIGURE 1.7 The porkpie.

FIGURE 1.8 The homburg.

FIGURE 1.9 The bowler/derby.

FIGURE 1.10 The trilby.

THE FEDORA

Fedoras were once considered de rigueur for men going out in public, whether they were headed to work or a ballgame. While once mainstream, a man in a fedora is now seen as a trendsetter. Fedoras are soft and usually made of felt, creased lengthwise down the crown and pinched on both sides. Fedoras will make you look manly and a bit mysterious. Worn by Prohibition-era gangsters, almost all of the movie stars of the 1940s and Old Blue Eyes himself, donning a fedora puts you in touch with a truly suave and manly heritage. **(FIGURE 1.6)**

THE PORKPIE

Named for its resemblance to an actual pork pie, this hat is similar to a fedora but with a flat top instead of a pinched crown. The brim is also shorter and turned up. The hat is often associated with the jazz, blues and ska culture, but was also worn by the likes of Robert Oppenheimer, father of the atomic bomb. **(FIGURE 1.7)**

THE HOMBURG

The homburg is another hat similar to the fedora. The homburg's brim lacks the fedora's pinches and is turned up all the way around. The hat is accented with a hatband into which a feather may be stuck. Less casual than a top hat and dressier than a fedora, the homburg was the go-to lid for politicians and diplomats in the twentieth century. Favored by the Godfather and resurrected by the likes of Snoop Dogg and Tupac, the homburg now carries a distinctly gangster flavor. **(FIGURE 1.8)**

THE BOWLER/DERBY

Bowlers are hard, made of felt and have very short brims. While considered a British icon, the bowler was also part of the urban culture of America in the nineteenth century. For example, one of the gangs that roamed the mean streets of New York City around this time was the Plug Uglies. The Uglies were never without their bowler hats, which they wore both as their signature piece and to protect their heads during their many scuffles with rival gangs. **(FIGURE 1.9)**

TRILBY

If the bowler is largely known as a British hat, the trilby is distinctively American. Trilbies, with their deeply indented crown and narrow brim, share similarities with the homburg and fedora but have a style all their own. Although traditionally associated with the jazz culture and paired with dressier outfits, today a checkered or tweed trilby is often worn to top off a more casual outfit. **(FIGURE 1.10)**

Wear a Hat With Confidence

"Cock your hat—angles are attitudes."

—FRANK SINATRA

Hats can give you a feeling of effortless cool and manly confidence. Few people loved hats more, or wore them better than Frank Sinatra. He was constantly playing with the idea of angling and tilting his hat to convey different attitudes. Here's how you can wear your hat to reflect your mood:

- Wear your hat pushed back to seem more open and accessible.
- Tilt your hat over your eyes to seem mysterious and intimidating.
- Tilt your hat up 1 inch from completely straight to project an all-business attitude.

Hat Etiquette

The hat is a singular accessory; when and where you don it, doff it and tip it conveys respect in a way no other piece of clothing can. In adopting the hat as your signature piece, you must also accept the responsibilities that go with it. Often ignored, hat etiquette will show that your uniqueness extends not only to your choice of headwear but to your manners as well.

Hats should always be removed:

FIGURE 1.11 Hats should always be removed when riding in an elevator in the presence of a lady.

- At funerals and graveside services
- Inside Christian churches
- During outdoor weddings
- Inside of homes, restaurants and buildings (unless in the corridors or lobbies of the latter)
- When riding an elevator in the presence of a lady **(FIGURE 1.11)**
- During the national anthem
- While eating meals (unless seated at the lunch counter of a diner)
- While conversing with someone

Tip your hat when:

- Greeting a friend (when greeting a lady friend, remove your hat completely by the crown)
- Excusing yourself to a woman whom you have inadvertently jostled or are passing by in a tight space
- Saying good-bye
- Expressing gratitude ("thank you" and "you're welcome")

The Perfect Hat for Your Ugly Mug

What we find attractive is largely based on symmetry. The more symmetrical a face is, the more appealing it appears to others. But there's not much we can do, short of surgery, to change the symmetry of our faces. There are ways to mitigate our asymmetries, however. You may have heard a woman in your life talk about getting a haircut that flatters her particular face shape. While dude haircuts don't come in enough varieties to have the same effect, there is another way guys can balance out their faces: hats. All hats make a man look more dapper. But picking a hat that is right for your face shape will increase your attractiveness and give you an even sharper appearance. If you've been inspired to bring back the hat, but weren't sure what kind of hat to get, this guide will help you pick the right hat for your ugly mug.

ANATOMY OF A HAT

Before we get started, let's do a quick rundown of some of the terms we'll be using to fit a hat to your mug.

"Taper" describes how narrow the top of the crown is compared to the bottom. Here's an example of a hat that tapers **(FIGURE 1.12)**. Notice how it gets narrower near the top of the crown.

Here's a hat that has no taper **(FIGURE 1.13)**. Notice how the crown doesn't narrow as it gets to the top.

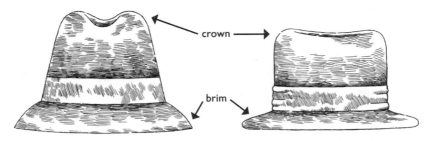

FIGURE 1.12 A hat that tapers gets narrower near the top of the crown.

FIGURE 1.13 A hat that has no taper doesn't get narrower at the top of the crown.

Now let's match a hat to that ugly mug of yours:

Short Full Face. Your face is shaped like: Jack Black. A round face tends to look short, so you want a hat that will give you a little height.

- Crown: Medium height and size
- Taper: Slight
- Hat Band: Narrow band of a contrasting color will add height
- Brim: Moderate width. Snap the brim to its full width and turn it up. Never snap it down or it will make your face appear shorter.
- Tilt: Back from face; tilting it over your face will make the face appear shorter.
- Recommended Hats: fedora, gambler, panama

Long Thin Face. Your face is shaped like: Will Arnett. Look for a hat that shortens the appearance of your face.

- Crown: Shorter height. Avoid crowns that are square, full or too high.
- Taper: Moderate
- Hat Band: Wide (will make your face shorter) with a contrasting color to break up your vertical lines
- Brim: Moderately wide, snapped from ear to ear
- Tilt: To the side with a slight back tilt
- Recommended Hat: fedora, homburg, derby

Top-Heavy Face. Your face is shaped like: Jon Favreau. The top-heavy face is wider on the top half and tapers to a narrower chin line. You want a hat that will balance out the top and bottom.

- Crown: Medium to short height, pinched toward the front. Avoid crowns that are full or too high.
- Taper: Moderate taper
- Hat Band: Medium to narrow, in a color similar to the color of the hat
- Brim: Medium width, rolled at back and sides, flat in front
- Tilt: To the side and not too far back on the head or you'll show too much of your wide forehead
- Recommended Hat: fedora, homburg

Square Face. Your face is shaped like: Orlando Bloom. Pick a hat that will add some curvature to your face and make it appear less boxy.

- Crown: Medium height, full and round
- Taper: Minimal to nonexistent
- Brim: Wide width, fully snapped or turned up
- Tilt: A side tilt will break up your square face lines. Don't push it too far back on your head.
- Recommended Hat: homburg, bowler

Long Nose. Your nose resembles: Adrien Brody, although perhaps not *that* long. Pick a hat that will break up the line from the brim to the tip of your nose.

- Crown: Medium height and not pinched too tightly at the front
- Taper: Minimal to nonexistent
- Hat Band: Wide and colorful
- Brim: Wide width, you want it to extend beyond the tip of your nose
- Tilt: To the side
- Recommended Hat: fedora

Prominent Jaw. You've got a chin like: Aaron Eckhart. Pick a hat that will balance your strong chin.

- Crown: Medium or low height, avoid crowns that are full or too high. Pick one with side dents; this adds just the right amount of fullness.
- Taper: Slight
- Brim: Medium width, snapped fully across. Make sure it doesn't turn up in the back sharply or it will make the jaw appear even more prominent.
- Tilt: Level, with a side tilt
- Recommended Hat: fedora

Receding Chin. You've got a chin like: Paul Dano. Pick a hat that will draw attention upwards, away from the chin.

- Crown: Low height
- Taper: Significant
- Hat Band: Narrow
- Brim: Flat or very shallow snap
- Tilt: Level with significant side tilt
- Recommended Hat: porkpie, trilby

Prominent Ears. Your ears stick out like: Will Smith. If your ears are large or stick out, pick a hat that will cover them.

- Crown: Full and moderately tall
- Taper: Minimal to slight
- Brim: As wide as possible in order to cover the ears and make them seem smaller. Flat or fully snapped. Do not roll the brim as this will highlight the ears.
- Tilt: Down in the back
- Recommended Hat: gambler, panama, wide-brimmed fedora

ATTENTION TO DETAILS

Even if you don a nicely fitted suit, tuck a piece of colorful fabric into your pocket and tie your tie with precision. If you don't pay attention to the details of your appearance, your whole look and first impression will be ruined. There are three things to check before you head out for a night on the town or a job interview: Are your clothes ironed? Are your shoes shined? Do your socks, shoes and belt coordinate with your suit? Refining these finishing touches will leave you looking like a SQUARE-RIGGED gentleman.

Ironing Your Clothes

Preparing for Ironing. Hang up your clothes immediately after drying. This will reduce the amount of wrinkles in your clothing (and consequently the amount of work you have to do with the iron).

Fill 'er up. Fill the iron with water so you have plenty of steam to get those wrinkles out. Set the iron to the appropriate temperature. Different fabrics require different iron temperatures. If the iron is too hot or steamy, you'll ruin the fabric. Check the tag on the inside of your clothing to find the appropriate setting. Generally, for all cotton fabrics, set the temperature on high; set it lower for part (or all)

synthetics. If you have both synthetic and cotton fabrics to iron, start with the synthetics, so you won't have to wait for the iron to cool down after tackling the cotton.

Iron on a padded surface. It makes ironing easier. If you don't have an ironing board, lay a towel over a desk. **(FIGURE 1.14)**

Dampen the garments. The key to good ironing is to start with slightly damp clothes. Take your shirt or pants out of the dryer before they completely dry. If your clothes are already dry, spray them down with some water until slightly damp.

IRONING A DRESS SHIRT

You don't want to approach ironing haphazardly. It's not efficient or effective. This is a battle against wrinkles. Like any hard-fought battle, you need an attack plan if you want to come out on top. Iron your shirt in this order to get the best result possible.

FIGURE 1.14 Iron on a padded surface. It makes ironing easier.

1. Collar: Lay it flat, wrong side up, pressing from the points toward the center. Then press it on the right side.
2. Yoke: The yoke is the panel that covers the shoulders. Lay it over the widest part of the ironing board to do the job.
3. Cuffs: Unbutton the cuffs and open them fully. Iron the insides, then the outsides.
4. Sleeves: Using the seams as your guide, smooth the sleeve flat with your palm and iron it; then flip it over and do the other side. Now iron the other sleeve.
5. Back: Lay it on the wide part of the ironing board, too.
6. Front panels: Start with the pocket, then do the panels. The little point of the iron helps you press around buttons.
7. Retouch: Retouch the collar and cuffs if they need it.

IRONING A PAIR OF PANTS

Just as with your shirt, if you want to get the absolute best results, you need to iron your pants in a certain order.

1. Turn the pants inside out and iron the waistband, pockets, fly area, seams and hems.
2. Turn the pants right side out and pull the waistband over the pointy end of the ironing board as if you were dressing it. Iron the waistband area and the upper part of your pant.
3. Pull the pants off the ironing board. Hold them by the hems and line up the outer and inner seams together. Lay the pants along the ironing board lengthwise.
4. Bring the hem of the top pant leg toward the waistband. Iron the inside of the bottom pant leg from the hem to the crotch. Turn the pants over and repeat for the other leg.
5. Line up the pant legs on top of each other. Iron the outside of the top leg. Flip the pants over and repeat on the other pant leg.
6. Hang them up immediately, but don't just throw them on the hanger. To maintain that crease you so meticulously created, you want

to hang your dress pants neatly. Grab the pants by the hem and find the crease. Bring the pants legs together and hold them together at the creases. You should see a nice straight line going down both sides of the pants. Once you have the pants lined up with a nice crease, take the hanger in one hand and slide it down the pants leg to about the middle. Gently fold the hem across the hanger.

Give Your Shoes a Mirrored Shine

For a shoe so shiny that you can see your reflection in it, all you need is a soft cloth, a can of Kiwi shoe polish and a good shoe brush.

1. To remove any dirt/mud/salt on your shoes, brush them off or rinse them under cold water.
2. Wrap part of the cloth around your index finger. Moisten the cloth at the fingertip with a small amount of water (do not soak the entire rag). Some people swear by spit, others by lukewarm water, still others by cold water. Experiment and see what works best for you. Rub your now-moist cloth in the polish to acquire a small amount. Make sure you match the color of shoe polish to the color of your shoe as precisely as you can. Do not dig divots in your polish, as it will create more surface area and cause it to dry out quicker, thus ruining a good can of polish.
3. Apply the polish in small circles, in very small amounts. Work one piece of the shoe at a time—toe, tongue, heel, inside upper and outside upper—until you have covered the whole shoe. This is your base coat.
4. Grab your shoe brush and brush the entire shoe vigorously.
5. Moisten your cloth and rub it in the polish again. Start buffing the boot/shoe by going over the entire shoe in small circles, with a light amount of pressure. Breathe "hot air" onto the boot/shoe as if trying to fog a mirror. This adds a slight amount of moisture to the boot and softens the outer layer of polish slightly, filling in the unseen

cracks and allowing the shoe/boot to become perfectly smooth and shiny. Continue until you get the preferred amount of shininess.

If you ever need a quick shine, just rub your shoe on the back of your pant leg. This is how Gramps did it in a pinch.

MANLY ADVICE

COLOR COORDINATING YOUR SOCKS, SHOES AND BELT

Socks: Sock color should match your pants, not your shoes. When you sit down and your socks are exposed, you want a solid line of color from your pants to your shoes. Socks that don't match your pant color create a jarring break in your outfit. So black socks go with black pants and brown socks go with brown pants. Absolutely and under no condition should you ever wear white socks with dark pants unless you want to look like Steve Urkel or Michael Jackson circa 1983.

Shoes: Coordinate your shoe color to your suit. First, the obvious: Wear brown shoes with brown suits, black shoes with black suits. Now the trickier: Wear black shoes with gray suits, brown shoes with blue suits.

Belt: Belt color should match your shoe color. Easy as pie, right?

GROOM LIKE A GENTLEMAN

For a gentleman, a little grooming goes a long way. Good grooming need not veer down the path of metrosexuality, fraught as that road is with the specter of eyebrow plucking and styling one's hair for hours in the hopes of getting that just out of bed look. The basics, a close shave and a sharp haircut, are all a man needs to face the world with confidence.

Why Every Man Should Go to a Barbershop

Men have stopped going to barbershops, and this is a man travesty of the highest order. A man should get his haircut only at a barbershop for the reasons I shall outline below:

A barber knows how to cut a man's hair. If you're like most men these days, you're probably going to some unisex chain salon like Supercuts. I used to do it, too. Most of the time, I'd walk out of those places with a crappy haircut. Sometimes my haircut would look decent for the first week or so, but then it would grow out into a horrible bowl.

The problem is that many of the people who work at salons are not trained barbers. They're cosmetologists. The difference between the two can spell the difference between a dopey-looking haircut and a great one.

A barber is trained to cut with clippers, the main tool in cutting a man's hair. Cosmetologists, on the other hand, are trained to use scissors. Their training is also geared toward catering to women's hair. They become experts in styling, coloring and perming–things a man has no need for. That's why when you ask the cute stylist at Supercuts to use the number two on the clippers, you walk away with a bad haircut. She's probably not well versed in how to use them. But a barber can employ the clippers with finesse.

It's a great place to chew the fat with other men. When I went to hairstylists, I hardly ever talked to the women who cut my hair. I'd chat about my family and theirs and that's about it. Women who cut my hair usually ended up chatting with the other women in the salon, while I sat there awkwardly.

Barbers, on the other hand, are interesting guys with fascinating stories to tell. And I in turn feel at ease to say what's on my mind. We converse about politics, cars, sports and family. Guys who are waiting read the newspaper and comment on current events. And everyone is involved: the barbers, the customers getting their haircut and the customers waiting to get their haircut.

Barbershops are among America's last civic forums. Where do people go today just to talk with others in the community? Coffee shops? Every time I go to a coffee shop, people are at their own tables minding their own business. The only other place that I can think of is a bar, but bars are now co-ed instead of being bastions of manliness. So if you want to get your thumb on the pulse of civic life in your community, head over to the barbershop. **(FIGURE 1.15)**

FIGURE 1.15 Barbershops are among America's last civic forums. If you want to get your thumb on the pulse of civic life in your community, head over to the barbershop.

You can get a great shave. Many barbershops still give traditional single blade razor shaves. You haven't lived until you've experienced the pleasures of a great shave at a barber. It's a relaxing, luxurious experience and will give you the best shave you've ever gotten. Plus, allowing another man to hold a razor to your neck is a good way to remind yourself that you're alive.

It's a great activity to do with your father or son. Men need traditions that can help bond them. Visiting the barbershop with your father or son is a great tradition to begin in your family. Many men have been going to the same barber all their life and have introduced their sons to the same chair and the same barber.

You'll feel manlier. I don't know what it is. Perhaps it's the combination of the smell of hair tonics and the all-man atmosphere. But more so, it's the awareness of the tradition of barbershops. Barbershops are places of continuity; they don't change with the shifts in culture. The places and barbers look the same as they did when your dad got his hair cut. It's a straightforward experience with none of the foo-foo accoutrements of the modern age. There are no waxings, facials, highlights or appointments. Just great haircuts and great conversation.

When you walk out of the barbershop with a sharp haircut, you can't help but feel a little manly swagger creep into your step. So next time you spot that familiar red-and-white striped pole, stop in. You'll be glad you did.

SHAVE LIKE YOUR GRANDPA

Proper shaving has become a lost art. Today's average male is completely in the dark about the fine art of the traditional wet shave their grandfathers and some of their fathers used to enjoy. Instead, they're only accustomed to the cheap, disposable, mass-marketed shaving products that line the shelves of today's drugstores. I'm not sure when or why it happened, but the tradition of passing down the secrets of a clean shave faded away. Thankfully this glorious male ritual is making a comeback.

Benefits of the Classic Wet Shave

Reduced costs. An eight-pack of your typical four-blade cartridge razors can set you back over twenty dollars. Twenty dollars! That's $2.50 per cartridge. The cost of a double-edged safety razor is no more than twenty-five cents, so you can save some serious money by switching over. Additionally you can save some dough by using traditional shaving creams and soaps. Not only will a can of the chemically packed gel goop that most drugstores sell cost you up to five dollars a can, it doesn't last long nor give you a quality shave. On the other hand, traditional shave creams and soaps are made from natural ingredients. While their initial cost may be a bit more than shaving gels, you'll need less product to get a proper lather. Thus, you end up saving in the long run.

Reduced environmental impact. Traditional wet shaving with a double-edged safety razor produces less waste than shaving with cartridge razors. The only waste is a single metal razor blade and lather down the sink. Unlike today's razor cartridges, a double-edged blade can easily be recycled. The tubes and bowls that most traditional shave creams and soaps are sold in produce less waste than those clunky non-biodegradable aerosol canisters that gels come in.

Better, more consistent shaves. Most men today walk around not knowing they have horrible shaves. Electric razors and the latest five-blade super-duper nanobot contraptions irritate the skin more than necessary, leaving razor burn, ingrown hairs and redness. Shaving with a safety razor will eliminate the skin irritation and give your face a clean, healthy look. With a safety razor, you're just using one blade instead of several that chew up your face while cutting your whiskers.

You'll feel like a badass. It's nice taking part in a ritual that great men like your grandfather, John F. Kennedy and Teddy Roosevelt took part in.

The Tools

Safety razor. Switching from a cheap disposable razor to double-edged safety razor is like upgrading from a Pinto to a Mercedes. A safety razor is a machine. It's nice holding a piece of heavy, sturdy metal in your hand while you're shaving, as opposed to a piece of cheapo plastic.

You can find safety razors in a variety of places. First, ask your grandpa if he still has one lying around. Chances are he does. If Gramps doesn't have one, try checking antique stores. I found my 1966 Gillette Superspeed Safety Razor in an antique store in Vermont. I paid only ten dollars for it. If you don't have any luck there, stop by eBay and do a search for safety razors. You're bound to find a few there. Finally, if buying a used safety razor doesn't fancy you, you can always buy a new one from one of several companies that still make them. A highly recommended safety razor is from Merkur. They have several types to choose from at varying prices. Look to spend about forty dollars for a new safety razor.

Blades. You can choose from a variety of different blades. Each blade has a unique sharpness and cutting ability. Experiment with different kinds until you find the ones you like.

Shaving brush. If you've never used a brush during shaving, you're in for a treat. A brush helps hydrate the shaving cream in order to form a thick, rich shaving lather. Using a brush to lather up helps get the shaving cream up under each whisker which results in better, smoother shaves. Plus, lathering up with a brush just feels nice on your face.

Brushes are made out of two types of animal hair: boar and badger. Boar bristles are stiffer, hold less water and are cheaper than badger bristles. You can find a boar hair brush at Wal-Mart for about four dollars. If you really want to have a nice shaving experience, splurge and buy a badger hair brush. Badger brushes create more lather and feel a lot nicer on your face.

Soaps and creams. If you're like the average guy, you've probably been getting your shaving cream from a can. This blue/green, chemically laced goop does nothing for your face and smells like a hospital. Traditional shave creams and soaps on the other hand are full of natural ingredients that nourish your face and leave you smelling absolutely manly. While these high quality creams and soaps may cost more than the can stuff, just a dab creates copious amounts of lather.

The Technique

Prep your beard. If you want a clean shave, you need to prep your beard adequately. The goal during beard prep is to soften your whiskers so shaving is easier and causes less irritation. The best way to soften your beard is to shave right when you get out of the shower. The hot water from the shower should hydrate and soften your beard enough for shaving. If you haven't showered, at least wet your whiskers with some hot water. A hot towel is also a great way to soften stubble.

Lather up. Take a small dollop (about the size of nickel) of shave cream and place it in a mug. Take your brush that you've presoaked with water and swirl the cream around until you get a nice thick lather. Apply the lather with your brush in swirling motions. When your face is covered, take a few strokes to smooth everything out.

Shave. Unlike shaving with cartridge razors, shaving with a safety razor actually requires some skill and technique. Once mastered,

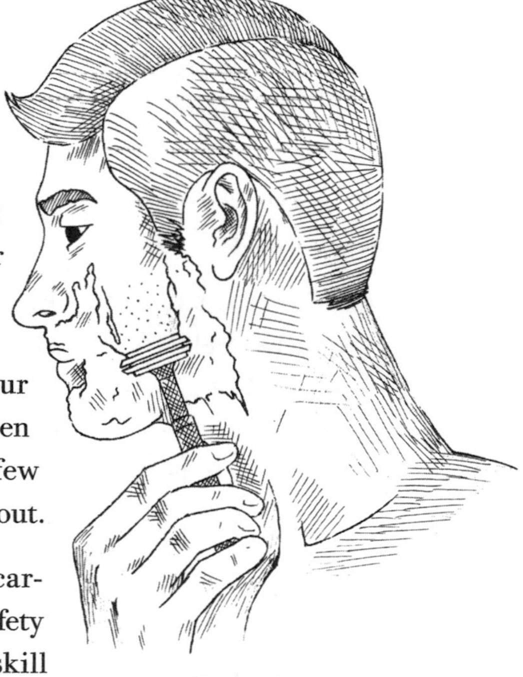

FIGURE 1.16 Shave with the grain of your beard to avoid slicing your face.

though, you should be shaving effectively in no time. The four keys to a successful shave with a safety razor are:

1. Use as little pressure as possible. You don't need to use pressure because the weight of the safety razor is sufficient to cut your beard. If you press down, you'll end up hacking up your face. To help counter the tendency to apply pressure, try holding the razor by the tip of the handle.

2. Angle the blade as far away from your face as possible. Angling your razor is probably the trickiest part. The proper angle is somewhere around 30 and 45 degrees. To get the proper razor angle, put the top of the razor head directly on your cheek, with the handle parallel with the floor. Now slowly lower the handle until the blade can cut your whiskers. Practice on your arm if you're not comfortable practicing on your face.

3. Shave with the grain. While shaving against the grain can get you that smooth feel, you risk slicing your face and causing ingrown hairs. When you're first starting out, shave with the grain of your beard. If you lather up and pass the razor more than once over your face, you're guaranteed to get a smooth finish. **(FIGURE 1.16)**

4. Go for beard reduction, not beard removal. The goal with shaving should be gradual beard reduction, not beard removal in one deft swoop. Most men try to get rid of their beard in one pass of the razor. This hack-and-go technique is what causes the majority of skin irritations. If you want to avoid skin irritation, lather up and pass the razor over your face several times. Your face will thank you.

These steps will take some getting used to if you have used cartridges your entire life. Keep practicing. It will begin to feel more and more natural and your shaves will greatly improve over time.

Post shave. Rinse your face with some cold water to close your pores. Treat your face to a nice aftershave. Aftershave helps reduce any irritation that may have occurred and will leave your skin looking healthy and smelling manly.

Don't forget. When you're done shaving your face, check to see if you have any nose or ear hairs that need trimming. No woman wants to see those daddy longlegs dangling from your nostrils. If your foliage is in need of pruning, use small scissors or an electric trimmer specifically designed for this purpose. And proceed carefully; you don't want to puncture an eardrum in the attempt to de-grandpaize yourself.

MANLY ADVICE

BUILDING THE PERFECT DOPP KIT

When a gentleman travels, he takes with him the things he needs to look sharp and well groomed away from home. Unlike many women who require a small suitcase for their toiletries, a traveling man needs only a few essentials to be happy. Nevertheless, a man needs a place to stow these items. Enter the Dopp kit.

THE BAG

The first thing you'll need is the bag. These aren't difficult to find. You can get a nylon travel bag for under five dollars at any big box store. They'll get the job done.

But if you want a Dopp kit with class, leather is the only way to go. Sure, it will cost you more, but it will last forever, age nicely and become something you enjoy owning and toting around. It's something you'll be able to pass down to your sons and grandsons, along with the stories of the places you took it.

THE SUPPLIES

After you have your bag, it's time to fill it up with the stuff you need to keep yourself well groomed while traveling. Most of things we suggest are common sense, others you might not have thought of but will be happy to have on hand during your adventures.

- Deodorant
- Soap and shampoo (if you're not staying at a hotel)
- Toothbrush, toothpaste, floss
- Shaving supplies: razor, brush and cream
- Nail clippers
- Lip balm
- Band-Aids
- Safety pins
- Aspirin
- Antidiarrheal medicine
- Lint roller
- Twenty-dollar bill
- Extra pair of contact lenses
- Comb
- Q-tips

BEHAVE LIKE A GENTLEMAN

In our increasingly open and casual society, the rules of etiquette are sometimes thrown in the wastebasket with other things deemed hopelessly formal and outdated. It is true that some aspects of etiquette are based on cultural customs and lack permanence: Kissing your female boss's hand will earn you the stink eye, not her favor. But much of what constitutes good manners is based on the sound and unchanging principles of consideration and respect. A gentleman is polite not because he is afraid of a scolding from Miss Manners, but rather because he is sensitive to the feelings and needs of others. He treats those around him with respect, and in so doing, encourages them to act likewise. And cultivating good manners is not a solely altruistic endeavor either; being a man a lady can take home to Mom and an employee a boss need not worry about causing embarrassment at an important lunch is a significant bonus.

HOW TO BE THE PERFECT PARTY GUEST

Throwing a party is a stressful endeavor. A host must worry about the food, the entertainment and whether their guests are getting along, having a good time and behaving themselves. Take one worry off the host's list by being a winning and polite guest. Not only will you help your friend's event be a success, you'll find more invitations to parties in your mailbox.

Always, always, RSVP. "RSVP" stands for "Répondez s'il vous plait," French for "please respond." When you receive an invitation that asks you to RSVP, the host or hostess is kindly requesting that you let them know whether or not you will be attending their function. Today's guests have come to see the RVSP as optional. Some men believe you need to call only if you are coming; some think you need to call only if you are not coming; and some do not think you have to call either way. Sometimes RSVPing is avoided because you don't want to face the awkwardness of telling someone you are not coming and making up an excuse about why.

However, not RSVPing is rather rude. The reason you must RSVP is that the host or hostess needs to know how to plan his or her party. They must pick the proper venue to accommodate a certain number of guests, the proper amount of party supplies, and perhaps most importantly, the right amount of food and beverages to serve the guests. By not RSVPing you keep your host completely in the dark as they attempt to prepare for their function. The host is forced to either overspend on supplies or be under-prepared for their event.

On that note, do not RSVP and then pull a no-show. Again, the host will have allotted for too much food and party favors, and these things will go to waste.

If you are attending a dinner party, offer to bring something. Cooking up a tasty meal for several guests is no easy task. Take some of the pressure off by offering to bring the salad or dessert.

Always arrive on time. If you're twenty minutes late, you will significantly add to the cook's stress by having them worry not only about the taste but whether the food is getting cold. If the food is not ready by the time you arrive, you simply have more time to mingle.

If the party is a large "come and go as you please" type of shindig, being "fashionably late" is acceptable.

Bring the phone number with you on the way over. If you get lost or have an emergency, you will need to call the host to keep them abreast. Don't keep the party waiting without any word from you.

Bring a gift for the host. A bottle of wine or a bouquet of flowers are excellent choices. This is particularly appropriate for dinner parties.

Come prepared for conversation. Don't be a party dud. On the way over, think of a few things you can talk about—movies you've seen, funny stories from work, and interesting news about yourself and your mutual friends. Think about the host and the other guests; what are they interested in and what kinds of questions can you ask them? Remember, you should almost always avoid controversial subjects such as politics and religion.

Eat and drink responsibly. Don't come to the party SAVAGE AS A MEAT AXE, ready to devour anything and everything in sight. At a party in which hors d'oeuvres are being passed around, don't put a ton on your plate. You'll look like a hog. And no double dipping! Finally, don't become inebriated.

Compliment the host. Tell the host what great food or what a great party it is at the midpoint of the night and then again when you are saying your good-byes.

Don't overstay your welcome. The appropriate time to leave is something you just have to feel in your bones. Things will be winding down, and conversation will hit a lag. At this point say, "Well, we've had a wonderful time tonight. I think we should get going. Thank you very much for having us."

Write a thank-you note. Within a few days of the party, always send a note of thanks to the host or hostess.

TABLE MANNERS FOR GENTLEMEN

While the rules of etiquette have largely disappeared from the public sphere, there is still an arena where your gentlemanly conduct will be put to the test: the dinner table. In the act of breaking bread, a man is revealed as a refined gentleman or an uncouth cad. Following these rules will mark you as someone anyone would be proud to have as a dinner guest.

1. Unless you are expecting a call that your wife's water has broken, be sure your cell phone is turned off before sitting down to a meal.

2. If you are accompanying a lady to dinner, pull out her chair for her and allow her to be seated first. **(FIGURE 1.17)**

3. When you sit down, immediately place your napkin upon your lap.

FIGURE I.17 If you are accompanying a lady to dinner, pull out her chair for her and allow her to be seated first.

4. If you see multiple eating utensils set before you, do not panic. The rule to remember is to work your way from the outside to the inside. Here's the nitty-gritty from there:

   - Smallest fork: for eating seafood
   - Next smallest fork: for eating salad
   - Biggest fork: save for dinner
   - Small spoon: for coffee
   - Big spoon: for soup

5. Wait until you know whether grace will be said before diving into the food. No man wants to be caught with a mouth full of roll as everyone else bows their head.

6. Keep your elbows off the table.

7. Always say please when requesting a dish be handed to you.

8. Among good friends and family, it is okay to request a taste of another's entree. But do not attempt to taste everyone's food at the table.

9. When eating rolls or bread, put a pat of butter on your roll plate and pass the butter on. Then, do not butter the entire roll at once, but instead tear off a slice or piece, butter that segment, eat it and repeat.

10. Do not eat too fast. Chew slowly and savor your food. Make time for conversation in between bites. Match your pace with that of your dining companions.

11. Never chew with your mouth open. And naturally do not attempt to speak when it is full either. Finally, the "see-food diet" joke is only appropriate for five-year-olds.

12. If you have a mustache or beard, be sure to avoid getting food lodged in your hairy masterpiece. Mustaches should not literally be used as soup strainers.

13. If dining at a friend's home and you find a hair in the food, quietly and inconspicuously remove it. Continue eating. If said situation happens at a restaurant, you may let the waiter know.

14. If you wish to consume the last item or portion of a dish, ask your fellow diners if anyone would like some before you polish it off.

15. Do not bring up unappetizing stories at the table. Your story about breaking open your head in a skateboarding accident may slay them at the frat house, but it will ruin the tomato soup at dinner.

THE DOS AND DON'TS OF CONVERSATION

We spend a great portion of our lives talking, whether in making small talk at parties, mingling around the watercooler at work, chatting with our date or discussing deeper issues with our friends. Through conversation we can win friends or alienate them, gain information and impart it, secure a job or lose one, improve our reputation or damage it. The difference between being a superior conversationalist and not is the difference between being the life of the party and being the ill-bespoken boor. The ability to engage others in winning conversation is an indispensable one and one of the keys to social and professional success. These guidelines, and continual practice, will have you on your way to becoming a master conversationalist.

The Don'ts

Don't continually look around the room as you have a conversation with someone. You may simply be curious about who is coming and going, but it will appear that you are not interested in the present conversation and are looking for someone else with whom to converse.

Don't continually glance at your watch or fidget. Don't appear to be bored while engaged in a conversation. **(FIGURE 1.18)**

Don't speak with only one person when mingling with a group. This will leave the others in the group standing there awkwardly. Engage each person with eye contact and questions.

Don't assume you are on the same page as a person you have just met when it comes to weighty issues. You should avoid issuing statements laden with value judgments. For example, don't say, "Isn't it wonderful that so-and-so won the election," without knowing the person's political sympathies.

Don't engage in gossip. If others do, always defend the person being spoken of.

Don't engage in one-upping or bragging. The latter is especially important if you are much better-off than the person with which you speak. The man who is a poor graduate student does not want to hear every detail of your luxury cruise to Rio de Janeiro.

Don't talk about inside jokes or "remember whens." If you find yourself in a group which consists of a close friend and new acquaintances, do not alienate the latter by engaging your friend on conversation topics with which the others have no understanding and nothing to add.

Don't use profanity. Some people don't mind. Some do. Better to stay on the safe side and come off as a polished gentleman.

Don't bore people with topics of conversation that are marginally interesting to the general public. You may find the intricacies of molecular biology to be quite scintillating, but most people do not.

Don't fill your conversation with complaints and criticism. No one wants to hang out with a GRUMBLETONIAN. The man who issues a constant stream of negativity will be avoided.

FIGURE 1.18 Don't continually glance at your watch or fidget. Don't appear to be bored while engaged in a conversation.

Don't intentionally use big words. Dropping "opprobrium" into conservation doesn't make you sound smart; it makes you sound pretentious. If you're intelligent, it will shine though in what you say without the artificial garnishes.

Don't relate intensely personal stories to new acquaintances, otherwise known as the over-share. You may think that such unburdening will create a faster bond, but it will more likely make the other person feel awkward.

Don't speak on controversial topics. Don't bring up subjects which are bound to cause contention. If others do, don't engage them and create a tense dispute.

Don't monopolize the conversation. Don't hold the floor for more than a few minutes at a time. Let others have their turn.

The Dos

Do make the person feel as though they are the most important person in the room. Lock into the conversation with great interest. Keep steady, but non-creepy eye contact, nod your head, listen intently and add *hmmmms* and *ahhhhs* when appropriate.

Do ask the person questions. Avoid talking about yourself too much. People like those who seem genuinely curious about their lives and interests.

Do allow an opening for the person to move on and mingle with others if they wish. You don't want to make someone feel trapped in conversation with you.

Do always keep an arsenal of entertaining stories at your disposal. When an awkward silence arises, don't make it worse by standing there staring into your cup. Be prepared with a myriad of topics with which to speak on.

Do wait for someone to finish speaking before adding to the conversation. Nothing is quite so rude as the man who cuts off others to get a word in.

Mi Casa Es Su Casa: Showing True Hospitality

The ability to show hospitality has been a measure of one's character across cultures and time. Hospitality goes beyond providing simple room and board; it involves making your guest feel comfortable, welcome and at home. Following a few simple guidelines will ensure your guest's visit will be a happy memory they will have forever.

Be on time to pick up your guest. No one wants to stand at the airport like a dope with no one to greet them. Make your guest's first impression of their trip a pleasant one by being there to warmly greet them as soon as they arrive.

Stock up on tasty treats. Your guest is on vacation; they want to relax and eat delicious BELLY TIMBER. Don't leave them at your house with only an old jar of mayo in the fridge. Make sure there's plenty of snacks to be had.

Make your abode as clean and pleasant as possible. After a long trip, there's nothing like stepping into a host's inviting home. You may not mind living in a mess, but that's no condition in which to have a guest. Make sure the guest room is particularly hospitable with an inviting bed and clean sheets. Even if your guest is sleeping on the couch, make the couch look cozy and comfortable.

Cook for your guest. Preparing food for your guest is an ancient rite of hospitality. It doesn't matter if you're not much of a chef, the effort is what counts. And always make breakfast for your guest on the first morning of their stay. There's something quite welcoming about waking up to a home-cooked meal.

Plan interesting activities for your guest. You want your guest to have a memorable visit and the best possible time while they are with you. Show them all your favorite spots and take them on all your favorite excursions. But also research some activities you know will particularly appeal to your guests and their interests. Even if you cannot accompany your guests on these sightseeing trips, give them a list of ideas, maps, directions and everything else they need to go out and enjoy themselves.

Never act imposed upon. Every guest worries a bit that they are imposing on you. There's never a need to magnify this insecurity. Always act as though you could not be more pleased that your guest is staying with you. You shouldn't have to fake such a sentiment; while you may experience moments of annoyance, keep in mind that such visits are infrequent and that your guest will soon enough be returning to their distant locale.

HOW TO BE THE PERFECT HOUSEGUEST

"Courtesy is as much a mark of a gentleman as courage."
—THEODORE ROOSEVELT

Just as a host has important hospitality responsibilities, the proper guest has certain rules to keep as well. Hospitality is a gift and it should be accepted graciously. Here's how to show your gratitude and make your stay a welcome and pleasant one.

Send money for groceries. If your stay will be an extended one, and your host will be paying for your food while you stay, send a check ahead of your visit to cover the cost of groceries. If you wait to offer dough until you are there, your host will inevitably turn down the offer out of politeness. So just mail a check before your trip with a note about how excited you are to be coming. If your visit will be short, take your host out to dinner and pay for the meal instead.

Show up on time. If you tell your host that you're going to come in on Wednesday morning, show up at that time. If you're running late, make sure to call ahead and update your host on when you'll be arriving.

Bring a gift. To show your appreciation for the free lodging, bring a gift. It doesn't have to be big or expensive. Baked goods, flowers, bottles of wine or unique gifts from your home state are always appreciated. **(FIGURE 1.19)**

Keep your area neat. Before you leave each day, make sure to make the bed and straighten your room. Put your dishes in the dishwasher after you use them.

Pitch in with the chores around the house. Help prepare the meals, wash the dishes and take out the trash. A gracious host will never directly ask you to help, so just get in there and start lending a hand.

FIGURE 1.19 To show your appreciation for the free lodging, bring a gift. It doesn't have to be big or expensive.

Let your presence interfere as little as possible with your friend's normal routine, household duties and career. Your friend may of course wish to take time off to hang out with you, but you should never be the one to impose on their schedule. Do your best to conform your routine to the routine of the household, as to not get in the way or create an imposition.

Disclose your schedule. Let your host know your schedule every day and do all you can to stick to it. This will help your host plan when to serve meals and how late they need to stay up.

Do not ignore your friend altogether. If your friend lives in a destination city and the purpose of your trip is both to visit with your friend and to see the sights, you should not entirely eschew the former to pursue the latter. No one wants to feel like you are simply using them as a hostel. Do your sightseeing when your friend is at work, plan activities together for when they are not, and invite your host on your excursions.

Come with some ideas about what you want to do and see. While your friend will surely have many things they wish to do with you, they should not be expected to entertain you all day long.

Even if you don't find all the activities your host plans for you enjoyable, keep your disappointment to yourself. Part of visiting a friend is accompanying them on excursions they enjoy. Your friend is working hard to entertain you; let him know you appreciate his efforts.

Don't criticize your host's hometown. If you are say, a proud New Yorker paying a visit to your country cousin in Omaha, do not go on and on in unfavorably comparing their city to the Big Apple. Most people are proud of their hometown; be generous in your compliments of it.

Always ask. Remember, you're a guest. Even if someone tells you to make yourself at home, still ask before you start using things. It's just polite.

Don't overstay your visit. As wise old Ben Franklin said, "Fish and visitors stink after three days." Your host has things to do, and they can't put their life on hold forever.

Strip the bed before you leave. Your host will likely wash the bed linens after you leave. Help make their job easier by stripping your bed before you depart.

Write a thank-you note. Showing true hospitality is one of the greatest kindnesses a friend can bestow. Be sure to express your gratitude to them by sending a note of thanks soon after your trip.

THE ART OF THANK-YOU-NOTE WRITING

Gratitude is a virtue every man should cultivate. Yet gratitude means nothing if you haven't mastered the art of expressing it. A man should use every opportunity to express to those around him how much he appreciates their love, support and generosity. One of the key ways of expressing gratitude is the thank-you note. Unfortunately, many men today completely overlook this aspect of etiquette and consequently break the hearts of sweet little grandmas everywhere. Every gentleman should be knowledgeable of the whens and hows of writing thank-you notes. Being a frequent and skillful writer of them will set you apart from your uncouth peers.

MANLY ADVICE

WHEN TO WRITE
A THANK-YOU NOTE

• When you receive a gift. (Especially if the gift is from your Italian grandma. If you don't write a thank-you note, she'll put the moloch on you.)

- When someone performs an act of service for you.

- When someone goes above and beyond what is asked of them, whether at work or in a friendship.

- After a job interview.

- When you stay overnight at someone's home.

- When someone shows you around their town when you're vacationing there, regardless of whether you stayed at their home or not.

- When someone has you over for dinner.

- When someone throws a party or event for you.

- Anytime someone does something extraordinary that warms your heart. Don't be stingy with the thank-you note. There's never a wrong time to write one.

Some Ground Rules

Always write the note as soon as possible. Send it within two weeks of attending the event or receiving the gift.

Send it through the mail. E-mail thank-yous are certainly convenient, but they are not appropriate except in response to very small things. Some may say, "Well, a thank-you is a thank-you. Why does it matter what form it takes?" Sending a thank-you note through the mail shows effort. It shows that you took the time to put pen to paper, addressed an envelope and bought a stamp. It's tangible; recipients can touch it, hold it and display it on the mantle. It makes your thank-you far more sincere.

Use real stationery. Having to run to the store to buy a card every time you need to write a thank-you note will make you drag your feet about writing them. So invest in some nice-looking stationery. It doesn't have to be fancy; buy something with a neutral, conservative theme so that the cards can be used for a variety of occasions.

How to Write a Thank-You Note

1. Begin by expressing your gratitude for the gift/service. Your opener is simple: "Thank you very much for _____." If the gift was money, use a euphemism for it. Instead of "thank you for the dough," say "thank you for your kindness/generosity/gift."

2. Mention specific details about how you plan to use a gift or what you enjoyed about an experience. If you are thanking someone for holding an event like a party or dinner, be specific about what you enjoyed about it. If you are thanking someone for a gift, tell the note's recipient how you plan to use it. This is true even for a monetary gift; tell the giver what you plan to spend it on or what you're saving for.

3. For some recipients, add some news about your life. This isn't always appropriate; obviously if you're writing a thank-you note for say, a job interview, you don't want to tell them how you recently caught a two-foot bass. But if you receive a gift in the mail from people who see you infrequently and who would like to know more about what's going on in your life (read: your extended family), give a brief sketch about what you've been up to recently. You know Aunt Myrtle will love it.

4. Close by referencing the past and alluding to the future. If the person gave you the gift at a recent event, write, "It was great to see you at Christmas." Then say, "I hope we all can get together again next year." If the person sent the gift in the mail, and you see them infrequently, simply write, "I hope to see you soon."

5. Repeat your thanks. "Thank you again for the gift" makes the perfect last line.

6. Valediction. Valedictions are the words or phrases that come before your name. The hardest part of a thank-you note is often choosing a valediction that appropriately conveys the level of your relationship with the recipient. *Love* can sometimes seem too gushy, and *Sincerely* can seem too formal. If your affections fall somewhere between those two expressions, here are some neutral valedictions that can fit a wide variety of situations and relationships:

- Yours Truly
- Truly Yours
- Kindest Regards
- Warmest Regards
- Best Regards
- Respectfully

A GENTLEMAN'S GUIDE TO TIPPING

Why tip? The difference between regular jobs and many jobs that require tips is that they are service jobs, and they are called service jobs because they are directly serving you. They personally and intimately affect you. You do not have to tip people for doing their job per se. But you might think about tipping people for the following reasons:

That person's livelihood depends on our tipping. An unsettling number of people don't seem to realize that many service workers in the United States, like waitresses, do not get a typical hourly wage. They get paid something like $2.50 an hour. Tipping in these cases is not optional, but necessary.

To show your gratitude. Another word for tip is *gratuity*. Many people in service jobs are overworked, underpaid and unthanked. At your job when you do something right, your supervisor says "thank you" and "job well done!" Who says thank you to the trashmen? Tipping is a way to say "thank you" to those who rarely hear it.

Tipping ensures great service. This is especially true of people who perform service for you regularly. If you tip a barista at a coffee shop you frequent or a waiter at your favorite restaurant, they will give you even better service next time.

If the person went above and beyond the call of duty. You don't have to tip someone for simply doing their job, but if someone really goes the extra mile for you, a tip is a nice way to show your appreciation.

How Much Should You Tip?

(NOTE: Tipping guidelines differ from country to country. This guide is intended for those who will be tipping in the United States.)

TRAVELING

Housekeeping at the hotel. A good tip for housekeeping is between $2 to $5 per night.

Tour guide. Tip between $1 to $5 per person in your group.

Skycap or bellhop. $1 to $2 per bag they lug for you. If you're running late and the skycap books your luggage to your plane so you can get there on time, bump up the tip.

Doorman. Only tip the doorman at a hotel if he gives you a hot tip on the best places to eat or visit while in town.

PERSONAL SERVICES

Barber. Tip 15 percent of the cost of the haircut.

Barista/smoothie maker/ice cream scooper. Spare change is always appreciated. If the barista starts making your order as soon as you walk in so that its ready for you by the time you get up to pay, tip a little extra. If they sing a song when you give them a tip, tell them not to sing or you'll take the tip back.

Takeout. If you order takeout from a restaurant, make sure to tip the cashier a bit. While they weren't waiting on you hand and foot, they did have to bust their butt to get your order together and ready. If they help you take your order out to the car, tip a bit extra.

Car washer. Three bucks is good for a basic car wash. If they take extra time when detailing it, give 10 percent of the cost of the wash.

Garage parking. Two dollars for your car. When you valet park, tip the person who brings you the car, not the person who parks it.

Tow truck. It depends on what services the person provides. If they jump your car or change your tire, tip about $4. If they tow it, $5 is a good tip. If they are towing you away from a no parking zone, give them the finger.

Massage therapist. Give 10 to 20 percent of the total cost.

Nurse. Usually tipping nurses at hospitals is not permitted, but don't tell that to Kate's Italian grandma. She was a retired nurse and believed you should definitely tip nurses and other health assistants. Any time she was at the hospital you can guarantee she got the best service because she gave her nurse "la boost."

Tattoos/body piercings. Fifteen percent of the total cost. If the tattoo artist does an amazing job of capturing the image of your mother on your arm, tip extra.

DELIVERY SERVICES

Newspaper delivery. During the holidays, give them a card with $20. Kate's parents do this every year and as a result, they have their paper delivered straight to their door instead of just thrown on the driveway.

Pizza/meal delivery. Fifteen percent is customary. If the weather is bad, i.e., there's snow and ice or a tsunami, and you're risking the delivery guy's life so you don't have to risk yours, tip extra.

Furniture/large appliance delivery. Five dollars per person. If they stick around and help you assemble or rearrange your furniture, tip extra.

OUT ON THE TOWN

Waiter. The customary amount is 15 to 20 percent. If they do an exceptional job, pay more. If you come in with a large group, ask if gratuity is added into your check so you don't tip twice. (Of course, as a former waiter, I always appreciated when someone gave me a little extra in addition to the gratuity.) Be extra generous when you're on a dinner date with a new lady—she'll be sure to steal a glance at the tip line of your bill to see if you are a cheap loser or a real gentleman.

Bartender. Tip 15 to 20 percent. Again, if they do an excellent job give more. If you come during happy hour and down twenty $0.99 draws, don't just leave 15 percent. Bartenders have to bust their butts to get those things poured for you and deserve more than your change.

Casino worker. There are lots of people you could be tipping at a casino. First, you have cocktail waitresses. Fifteen percent is customary. Many people tip dealers when they have a successful run, ensuring the continuation of good karma.

Taxi driver. Standard tip is 15 percent. If they get you to your destination quickly, tip extra.

HOLIDAYS

During the holidays, it's customary to give a little more for the everyday services we receive. Here is a short list of people you should consider giving "la boost" to during the holidays.

Mail carrier. It's against federal law to tip federal employees, but they can accept gifts of less than $20. Most will probably look the other way if you give more.

Garbage/recycling person. These people have a dirty job. Recognize their work around the holidays by giving them a tip. Ten dollars per person is nice.

Teacher. If you have kids in school, it's customary to give their teacher a small gift at Christmastime. Here's a tip: Teachers get box loads of body lotion, candles and various apple-themed knickknacks (no, you're not the first person to think of giving them an apple-shaped paperweight). Give them something they'll really enjoy like a gift card to Borders or Target.

Babysitter. A gift in addition to their normal pay is nice. Gift cards are always appreciated.

Cleaning person. An extra week's pay or a nice gift.

MODERN TECHNOLOGY AND THE NEW RULES OF ETIQUETTE

Modern technology presents the contemporary gentleman with the kind of etiquette pitfalls Emily Post could never have imagined. Just as World War I was especially bloody because the artillery had progressed faster than the development of new military tactics, technology presents an unmannered minefield because etiquette has not kept pace with its development. You can help bring some civility to the modern age by adhering to the following guidelines.

The Cell Phone

"Good manners are made up of petty sacrifices."
—RALPH WALDO EMERSON

Don't talk on your cell phone when you have a captive audience. No one in the plane, train, restaurant, gym or store wants to be held hostage to your conversation.

FIGURE 1.20 Don't lose respect by walking around with a headset 24/7. Keep it in the car where it belongs.

Don't use your phone in any place in which people expect a certain atmosphere. There are certain situations in which people expect a respectful quiet to prevail. A cell phone should not burst this bubble of ambience. Thus, you should never use your cell phone at funerals, weddings, classes, church services, movies, plays, museums, etc. By even allowing your cell phone to ring, never mind speaking into it, you announce to the world that your conversation is more important than the ruminations of everyone else in the room. It is the height of arrogance.

Don't talk or answer your cell phone while talking to ANYONE in person. There are no exceptions to this rule. Don't answer it when you're talking to someone at a party. Don't answer it when you're eating at a restaurant. Don't answer it when you're making a purchase or ordering food; the server or clerk is not a robot; each is a human being deserving of your respect.

Don't use a Bluetooth headset unless you're driving. You've seen the "headset people". They look like they just walked out of *Star Trek*. Headsets distance and disconnect you from the people around you. Don't lose respect by walking around with a headset 24/7. Keep it in the car where it belongs. **(FIGURE 1.20)**

Do use a simple ring tone. Personalized ring tones are everywhere. But be aware of what ring tones say about you. Jenna Jameson's "Moan" tone shows you have no taste; pop music ring tones show that you are still in tenth grade. Stick with something simple.

Don't use text messages to convey important ideas. This includes texting to break up, to declare your love or to curse someone out.

Don't text in ALL CAPS or use multiple exclamation marks. If you're that excited, you should be calling the person, not texting.

Don't expect a response to your text message right away. And if you don't get one, don't text follow-up messages, asking the person if they received your first one.

Don't check your text messages while at dinner, checking out at a store or conversing with another person. The crack-berry habit is tough to break, but people deserve your undivided attention.

The Internet

The beauty of the Internet is that it allows for free-flowing communication in an unprecedented way. But in the euphoria of this new freedom, we have forgotten the importance of common courtesy. Greater accessibility to others does not negate the need for respect. Even when interacting as anonymous, disembodied versions of ourselves, the rules of civility still apply.

BLOGS AND FORUMS

Never say something to a stranger on the Internet that you would not say to a stranger in person. The Internet provides a cloak of anonymity behind which people feel free to say whatever they want. Yet the words which we both write and speak are our creations. We must take ownership of them. Never write something you would not be proud to have attached with your real name. Before you hit send, stop and ask yourself: "Would I use these words if this person was standing right in front of me?" If not, reword your communication.

Don't attack people personally. Blogs and websites provide forums for the respectful exchange of ideas. You should thus never personally attack the people behind those ideas. Blog users will sometimes make a valid comment, only to end with "You're an idiot!" And some will dispense with the valid argument part altogether. Using personal attacks adds nothing to the conversation and only shows that you do not have anything insightful or intelligent to offer.

Don't just tear things down. Many an Internet user's energy is devoted to poking holes in every idea that crosses their path. But cynicism is easy. Chronic debunkers don't do any of the hard work it takes to create something, and then they barely lift a finger to tear things down. There's nothing wrong with criticism, but be constructive with your comments. If you have nothing substantive to add to the conversation, then it's best to CHEESE IT.

Don't use excessive vulgarity. Nothing shows a juvenile mentality and a lack of class like excessive vulgarity. While salty language has been on the rise in normal conversation as well, the proliferation of profanity on the Internet is excessive. Because of the information glut on the Internet, men feel they must pepper their comments with over-the-top language to keep them from being lost in the shuffle. But if such additions are needed to get attention, you clearly did not have anything meaningful to say in the first place.

E-MAIL

The modern gentleman knows how to deftly use e-mail. He recognizes that it is a tool to be used and is not a slave to checking it constantly. Gentlemen show their e-mail recipients the same respect they would give them if they were meeting face to face.

Be concise and to the point. Don't make e-mails longer than they should be. People use e-mail to save time, so writing your magnus opus in an e-mail message will probably irritate people. As a general guideline, try to keep e-mails shorter than five sentences.

Use proper spelling and grammar. Every piece of communication you send out to the world is a reflection of you. An e-mail filled with spelling and grammatical mistakes will leave a bad impression. It tells the reader that they're not important enough for you to run a simple spell check. Show your readers respect by proofreading your e-mails before you hit send.

Respond within twenty-four hours. If there's a question that you don't know the answer to and will take some time to research, go ahead and send a response saying you'll get back to them soon with the answer.

Answer all questions and preempt future questions. Failing to answer all the questions in an e-mail forces your contact to e-mail you again. Don't waste people's time by making them write another e-mail. Also, if appropriate, try to preempt other possible questions in your e-mail. It will save your correspondent time, and they'll appreciate your thoughtfulness.

Make it personal. Show your contact that you have them in mind when writing your e-mail. Address them by name and add information which will give your e-mail a personal touch.

Do not write in all capitals. Writing an e-mail IN ALL CAPS indicates shouting. This can irritate people, and you'll get a response you probably weren't looking for. Gentlemen don't shout in normal conversation, so don't do it in your e-mail either.

Don't overuse Reply to All. Use this function only if your message needs to be seen by each person who received the original message. If you use this function all the time, you will irritate people by filling up their e-mail box with needless responses.

Don't use abbreviations or emoticons. LOL! WTF! THX 4 UR HLP! You're not fifteen anymore so stop writing your e-mails like you are. A gentleman uses proper language when speaking and writing.

Don't forward chain letters or stupid jokes. Nothing says "I HAVE A BRAIN THAT FUNCTIONS AT SIX GUINEA-PIG POWER" like forwarding chain letters. Gentlemen recognize that e-mail chain letters are dumb, childish and a huge waste of time for the recipient.

Use discretion with what you put in an e-mail. Don't put anything that would embarrass you if it went public. In just one click, your reputation as a gentleman can be ruined.

FACEBOOK

Gentlemen only use Facebook. MySpace is for cads and scallywags.

Don't poke. Would a gentleman poke someone in real life? Of course not! So don't do it online. Poking is not an acceptable form of flirtation; neither are the other actions that some Facebook applications allow you to do. If you want to show someone you're interested in them, man up and send a private message to them. Better yet, call them.

Use discretion when wall posting. Do not use Facebook's wall to have entire conversations. You'll look like a boob if you do. Use wall posts for well wishes and hellos. Also, do not post anything too personal on a person's wall. Remember, walls are public spaces, so treat them as such.

Finally, use appropriate language when writing on someone else's wall. Avoid off-color comments and gossip. And check for spelling mistakes. Just think, "What kind of impression do I want to give others?"

Keep photos of yourself to a minimum. Especially photos taken of yourself by yourself, by holding the camera away from your face. A gentleman is modest and discreet. Hundreds of photos of yourself reveal your vanity.

Remove compromising photos of yourself. If you're a true gentleman, you shouldn't have to worry about any incriminating photos of you winding up on Facebook. However, if a photo of you in a compromising pose does slip by, ask the poster to take it down. At least remove the tag of you in the photo.

Do not break up with a woman through Facebook. Only a BEING WHO BELONGS TO THE CULT OF NON-VIRILITY would use Facebook's relationship status feature to break up with their girlfriend. If you are not man enough to look a woman in the eyes and tell her it's over, you weren't man enough to be in a relationship to begin with.

Take it easy on the applications. Don't overload your profile with unnecessary applications such as Superpoke, Food Fight, etc. Also, be careful with the kind of applications you install on your profile. A gentleman avoids applications that demonstrate a lack of judgment or maturity. That means no "Sex Position" or "Beer Wars" applications.

Join Facebook groups with discretion. The groups you choose to join, even as a joke, say a lot about you. Use discretion. Additionally, keep the number of groups you join to a minimum.

Don't "friend" someone you don't know or hardly know. Facebook has degraded the meaning of *friend*. A gentleman respects semantics and only includes people in his Facebook network that are truly his friends. Don't be afraid to say no to random people who try to befriend you.

Your favorites should be just that. Listing your favorites means listing the things you like the best not every single thing you've ever listened to, seen or read. Having a huge list of favorites shows you don't have enough taste to pick what things you like the best. Being ultra-inclusive doesn't make you seem cultured ... it makes you seem insecure.

Respond to people's Facebook wall posts and messages. Respond within twenty-four hours. If you feel overwhelmed with Facebook messages, let others know you prefer to be contacted by e-mail.

CHAPTER TWO

⊰|THE|⊱
FRIEND

"My father always used to say that when you die,
if you've got five real friends, you've had a great life."
—LEE IACOCCA

Friendships are an important part of a man's life. Friends are those men you can count on when the chips are down. They'll back you up even when the whole world is against you. Friends are those men who'll buy you a beer when you lose a job or your lady dumps you. Sadly the mighty bonds of man friendship have been greatly eroded during our modern age.

THE HISTORY OF MAN FRIENDSHIPS

Men who know no differently accept the current state of man friendships as inevitable. But a brief look at the history of male friendship shows otherwise and points the way toward recapturing the glory of brotherly bonds.

THE HEROIC FRIENDSHIP

In ancient times, men viewed male friendship as the most fulfilling relationship a person could have. Friendships were seen as nobler than marital love with a woman because women were seen as inferior. Aristotle and other philosophers extolled the virtues of platonic relationships—a relationship of emotional connection without sexual intimacy. Platonic relationships, according to Aristotle, were the ideal.

During this period of time, the idea of the heroic friendship developed. The heroic friendship was a friendship between two men that was intense on an emotional and intellectual level. Heroic friends felt bound to protect one another from danger. Examples of heroic friendships exist in many ancient texts from the Bible (David and Jonathan) to ancient Greek writings (Achilles and Patroclus).

MALE FRIENDSHIPS IN COLONIAL AND NINETEENTH-CENTURY AMERICA

Male friendships during the colonial period and nineteenth century were marked by an intense bond and filled with sympathy and sentimentality. Friendships between men, in many instances, had a similar intensity as romantic relationships between men and women. Essentially it was a continuation of the heroic friendship of the ancient world, coupled with the emphasis on emotion common to the Romantic Age. A fervent bond did not necessarily imply a sexual relationship; the idea that these ardent friendships in some way compromised their heterosexuality is largely a modern conception.

Men during this time freely used endearing language with each other in daily interaction and letters. And they weren't afraid to get all touchy-feely with one another either; many men would give no thought to draping their arms around their bud, sitting on one another's lap or even holding hands. It was also quite common for men to share a bed to save money. Men were free to have affectionate friendships with each other without fear of being called a queer because the modern concept of homosexuality and the strict straight/gay dichotomy did not yet exist. It wasn't until the turn of the twentieth century that psychologists started analyzing homosexuality. When that happened, men in America started to become much more self-conscious about their relationships with their friends and traded the close embraces for a stiff pat on the back. The man hug was born.

MALE FRIENDSHIPS IN TWENTIETH-CENTURY AMERICA

"The better part of one's life consists of his friendships."

—ABRAHAM LINCOLN

The man friendship underwent serious transformations during the twentieth century. Men went from lavishing endearing words on each other and holding hands to avoiding too much emotional bonding or any sort of physical affections whatsoever. Fear of being called gay drove much of the transformation. Ministers and politicians decried homosexuality as being incompatible with true manhood. (FIGURE 2.1) Additionally, the Industrial Revolution and the country's shift from an

FIGURE 2.1 During the twentieth century, the man friendship went from lavishing endearing words on each other and holding hands to avoiding any sort of physical affections whatsoever.

agrarian to a market economy affected the dynamics of all social relations. The resulting capitalistic culture, which gravitated to the new ideas of Social Darwinism and believed only the fittest would survive, influenced the way men viewed each other. Instead of being a potential friend, the man next to you became competition. In a dog-eat-dog world, it's hard to get ahead when the guys you need to snack on are also your bosom buddies.

Increased mobility during the twentieth century also contributed to the decline in male friendships. With more men following their work, it was hard to set down roots and make true friends. Man friendships did not die out of course, but the basis of the relationship shifted from a bond based on deep emotional connections to one centered on common pursuits. As leisure time increased and men moved to the suburbs, they formed their friendships on the golf course, at the neighborhood block party and in the corporate workplace.

The Future of Man Friendships

It's a shame that our society's ingrained homophobia prevents men from connecting with each other on a more emotional and physical level. American men are missing out on the benefits of close friendships. Studies reveal that men who have several close friends are generally happier and live longer than men who don't. And yet research shows that the number of friends and confidantes a man has has been steadily dropping for decades, leading to greater isolation and loneliness.

It's high time modern men took their place in the glorious history of man friendships. We hope this chapter will help you do just that.

BAND OF BROTHERS: ◀ MAKING AND KEEPING STRONG FRIENDSHIPS ▶

When a young man is in high school or college, making friends comes easily and naturally. Yet when his school years conclude, and especially when he gets married and moves, a man begins to find it quite hard to make new friends and maintain the bond with his old pals. At this point in life, cultivating his friendships takes a little more effort and work, but it is infinitely worth it.

Recruiting Your Band of Brothers

Fraternize at work. You spend more time with people at work than you do at home. And there are probably some dudes at work that you get along with swimmingly. Instead of keeping them in the *work* friend category, convert them into *friend* friends. Go for some drinks after work. Invite them over to your house to watch the game on Saturday. If you're married, go out for dinner with him and his spouse.

Meet your neighbors. It's not only serial killers who can accurately be described as "quiet men who kept to themselves." You can sadly live in a neighborhood for ten years and not know the people who live next door to you. But they might turn out to be your future best bud. So don't be a Dahmer. A great way to meet your neighbors is by hosting a party or attending neighborhood events like block parties. If you're feeling particularly brave, just go up and introduce yourself.

Join an organization. Part of the difficulty today's men face with making new friends is the isolated nature of their social lives. There's work and home, and not much else. Joining an organization is quite possibly the best way to create a social circle for yourself.

MANLY ADVICE

POTENTIAL ORGANIZATIONS TO JOIN

Fraternal Organizations. They're not just for your grandpa. Fraternal organizations are the perfect conduit for friendship making because they provide all the ingredients needed for brotherly bonding: common ideals, a sense of tradition and responsibility, and a focus on service. While there are several great fraternal organizations out there, it's hard to refute that the Masons are the best.

Churches/Religious Organizations. Like fraternal orders, churches are a fruitful place to make man friendships as they are a place where you can find gents with similar values and goals. Many churches have groups that are for men only and are designed for both fellowship and spiritual growth.

Sports Leagues. If you love sports, instead of spending your weekend alone watching them on TV, join an intramural league and get back on the field. From flag football to ultimate frisbee, your town is sure to have clubs that meet for some good old-fashioned man competition. Joining up will whip you into shape, feed your man spirit and give you the kind of bond with other men that can only be found on the playing field.

Toastmasters. Toastmasters solves two fundamental problems in the life of modern man: a lack of friends and a deficiency in the art of public speaking. Not only will you learn to be a better orator, you'll also meet lots of other men to befriend.

Book Clubs. For some reason (read: Oprah), book clubs have become associated with women, baring one's soul and Kleenex. But there's nothing sissy about books; discussing great literature was a pastime of many of the great men in history. Libraries sometimes offer male-only book clubs that read books men like. If your library doesn't, why not start one at your house?

KEEPING YOUR FRIENDSHIPS ALIVE

"Good fellowship and friendship are lasting, rational and manly pleasures."
—WILLIAM WYCHERLEY

Set a common goal. Men experience the greatest bond when they are working together toward a common purpose, i.e., when they become a band of brothers. The same is true whether you're storming Omaha Beach or simply living in the burbs. So set a goal to attain with your friend or a group of friends. Decide to run a marathon, quit smoking or lose weight. Don't forget to set up a system to ensure accountability.

Create a competition. Competition in life can drive people apart; a friendly competition among men can bring them together. Create a competition with your friends and set a friendly wager; something a bit embarrassing for the loser is always fun and will keep the group motivated. **(FIGURE 2.2)**

Take a mancation. Mancations are occasions for pure, uninterrupted male bonding. They can be as short as a weekend or as long as a week. The destination can be anywhere, but it should involve manly activities. The key to the mancation is to make it an immutable tradition. Set a time and make it an annual happening. You can plan the other things in your life around that nonnegotiable date.

Guys' night out. The cliché of the "guys' night out" involves a man ditching his unhappy wife and household chores to spend time with his boys. So let's be clear here: Your wife and her needs should always come first. At the same time, if you and she have spent ample time together, then guys' night out is quite appropriate. Encourage her to have a girls' night out as well. The quality of your relationship will improve as a result of having healthy friendships.

FIGURE 2.2 A friendly competition among men can bring them together.

STAYING IN TOUCH WITH YOUR BUDS

Any relationship, including the man friendship, needs communication to survive. Most guys aren't keen on having heart-to-hearts. Spending regular time together, even without much talking can be enough. But if you move to different locales, you'll have to make an effort to stay in touch. Guys generally don't enjoy talking on the phone, and we usually aren't big e-mail writers either. But there is a long-standing, centuries-old tradition that has kept man friends connected over whole lifetimes: letter writing.

Snail mail may have fallen out of favor with most of society, but it's key in maintaining healthy friendships. Sure e-mail is easy, but it's also easily ignored. We let it sit there and in a few days it has disappeared to another page and out of our brains. Letter writing is something altogether different: Real and tangible, it leaves your hands and physically plants itself in the life of your friend. There it is, a part of you, sitting on their kitchen counter. People can't throw stuff like that away. A letter practically requires an answer. Commit to writing your friend once a month; it will keep alive your bond no matter where life takes the both of you.

LEARN THE SECRET HANDSHAKE: ◀ JOIN A FRATERNAL LODGE ▶

You see their emblems next to the "Welcome to Anytown, USA" sign when you drive into any locale in America. You can recognize them by a lapel pin they might wear or a bumper sticker they have on their car. And without them driving around in go-carts and three-wheelers, Fourth of July parades as we know them today would cease to exist.

They are the thousands of men who belong to fraternal lodges.

While fraternal lodges like the Freemasons and Oddfellows are often the butt of jokes or fodder for conspiracy theories, fraternal lodges played an important part in the history of male socialization in America. Becoming a member of a fraternal lodge was once a common rite of passage for American men. It was a way for a man to make new friends, network with others and find meaning in their lives. Your grandpa probably belonged or still belongs to one. Sadly this once vibrant and manly tradition has been on the decline for several decades. But the fraternal lodge is due for a revival.

THE HISTORY OF FRATERNAL LODGES

"Friendship is the only thing in the world concerning the usefulness of which all mankind are agreed."

—CICERO

During the nineteenth century, the number of different fraternal lodges as well as membership in lodges exploded in America. The home, transformed by the period's so-called "cult of domesticity," had become an effeminate, doily-laden foo-foo abode, and men from all walks of life flocked to lodges as bastions of unfettered manliness. The lodge was a man hangout, where men could socialize, play pool, throw back a few and vigorously discuss the pressing issues of the day.

Membership in fraternal lodges continued to grow through the early part of the twentieth century, peaked during the 1930s but then quickly began to decline. Men began to find the elaborate rituals of fraternal lodges off-putting, found new sources of entertainment in radio, television and movies, and looked to organized sports and the emerging corporate culture for social opportunities. Additionally, increasing pressure and desire for men to spend more time with their families forced many men to give up lodge life.

Today many fraternal lodges are on the verge of extinction. Their ranks are getting older, and young men have very little interest in replacing them. It wouldn't be surprising if in a few decades fraternal lodges began to disappear completely.

Why Modern Men Should Join a Fraternal Lodge

This manly tradition need not fade away. Fraternal lodges aren't just for your grandpa. You, too, can take part in these manly institutions. Here are five reasons you should look past the silly hats and become a member of a fraternal lodge:

1. You'll be taking part in a storied tradition. This tradition is shared by some of the greatest men in history. George Washington, Isaac Newton, Ben Franklin and Theodore Roosevelt were all Masons. How awesome would it be to join the ranks of these great and noble men?

2. The ritual. Our modern world is sadly lacking in ritual. Even churches are dumping their rituals in order to be more hip and edgy. But ritual is an important part of the human experience. Through ritual we can learn important truths, explore the mysteries of the universe and quiet our busy minds. Also, if you feel like you lack a rite

FIGURE 2.3 Lodge brothers are extremely loyal to one another and will always have your back.

of passage into manhood, the ritual of fraternal lodges can provide one for you.

3. You'll make new friends. Sure, these new friends will probably be seventy-five years old, but who better to glean manly wisdom from? What's great about fraternal lodges is that they attract men from all backgrounds, but who all have the same goal of becoming better men. So you'll get to interact with a wide variety of people. Lodge brothers are extremely loyal to one another and will always have your back. **(FIGURE 2.3)**

4. You'll become a better man. While most fraternal orders require a belief in a Supreme Being (which is open to personal interpretation), very few require adherence to any set creed, church or political system. Instead fraternities exist to promote and inspire values that all men can get behind such as brotherhood, charity and loyalty.

5. You'll have an opportunity to serve your community. Most men want to give back but don't know where or how to do so. Fraternal lodges will give you the motivation and direction you need to get off the couch and start serving your fellow man. While lodges still provide social activities like sports leagues and parties, their main function these days is to plan and carry out service projects from Habitat for Humanity to pancake breakfast fund-raisers. Giving back to your community is definitely a manly thing to do. And you might even get to pop a wheelie in the local parade.

◄ HOW TO HELP A FRIEND WITH A PROBLEM ►

If you see your buddy going through a rough patch in life, it's only natural to want to offer some advice on how to remedy the situation. But helping a man friend with a problem can be a sticky situation; men don't like heart-to-hearts, they're often too prideful to ask for help and a marathon of watching *Sex and the City* reruns and eating pints of Ben and Jerry's won't soothe their troubles. So when helping your friend with a problem, you must walk softly and carry a fishing pole.

Go do something together. Men tend to be uncomfortable with baring their souls. So instead of sitting your friend down and gazing into his eyes, go jogging, take him fishing or bowling, or play some pool. It's easier to unburden yourself when you're sitting looking outward, instead of face-to-face. In between fishing casts, ask your friend about his problem. (FIGURE 2.4)

Get the facts. Before you can successfully help someone, you need to know all the facts about the problem. Harness your inner news reporter by asking who, what, when, where and why questions. And make sure you listen attentively while your friend speaks.

Enable your friend to discover the solution himself. Men are most likely to follow through with something if they feel like they thought of the idea themselves. And oftentimes a man simply needs to be able to think out loud to come up with the answer to his troubles. Therefore your job as a friend is to act as a facilitator. After you hear your friend's problem, ask him very nonchalantly, "So what do you think you can do to fix your situation?" Usually he'll start listing some things. When he says something that you think would be particularly effective, let him know and explore the idea further.

Ask if he wants your advice. If helping them figure out their own solution isn't going anywhere, *ask* your friend if he would like some advice. By asking before you jump into the fray, you respect your friend's manly pride. If they say no, then it's NO GREAT SHAKES. Just keep fishing or bowling and let your friend know you're always willing to talk about it in the future. Don't bug him about it; that's the man code.

FIGURE 2.4 It's easier to unburden yourself when you're sitting looking outward, instead of face-to-face. Go jogging, take him fishing or bowling, or play some pool.

Don't preach. Men hate being preached to. Don't put off a smug vibe that makes your friend feel you think you're better than him for being in this pickle. Skip the patronizing sermon of "shoulds" and "musts"; instead offer suggestions. Say, "This is what I would do if I were in your situation," "You could try doing X" or "I once had a similar problem and here's how I handled it."

Give 'em some straight talk. Men don't like to be preached to, but they do appreciate a justified kick in the pants. If your friend's been a DUNDERHEAD, then you need to call him on the carpet. Talk to him respectfully and honestly, man to man. Sometimes you have to tear a man down to bring him back up.

Naturally the specific situation should determine your approach. If the problem is more sensitive, like his girlfriend cheating on him, be more sympathetic.

The transition from the snuggling, hand-holding days of the nineteenth century to the less affectionate modern age has been a bumpy one, leaving man friends confused on how to properly show their affection. A firm, hearty handshake, always appropriate with acquaintances and business colleagues, falls quite short when dealing with one's bosom buddies. Yet, neither are most men looking to spoon the afternoon away. Thus, a man must know how to take the middle path: the man hug.

MANLY ADVICE

WHEN TO HUG

Women hug after their friend returns from a bathroom break. Men ration their hugs, doling them out only on certain occasions. These include:

- When you haven't seen a friend for a long time. This is measured in months, not days or weeks.
- When a friend shares a bit of good news such as the announcement that he has gotten engaged or impregnated his wife. (If he has impregnated someone other than his wife, substitute a man slap in lieu of a man hug.)
- The celebration of a beloved sports team's victory. Man hugs in this case can last far longer and be much more vigorous than normal.

HOW TO PERFORM THE INTERNATIONAL MAN HUG (FIGURE 2.5)

1. Stand face-to-face. Side hugging, in which one arm, or heaven forbid both arms, are wrapped around the shoulders or torso, and the head and cheek are pressed together is never appropriate.

2. Spread your arms wide to announce your intention of moving in for the hug. This allows your friend to prepare himself and raise his arms in turn. You don't want to catch him off guard and end up pinning his arms to his sides.

3. Commence the hug. Don't linger too long, just a couple of seconds will do. Don't lean your head into your friend's head or neck; this will come off as a nuzzle.

FIGURE 2.5 The International Man Hug.

4. Pat your friend on the back with an open hand or closed fist. As opposed to the feminine squeeze for emphasis, the slap is the distinguishing mark of a man hug.

5. Release the hug. Pull your hands and arms briskly away as to avoid the impression that you are caressing your friend as you exit the embrace.

How to Perform the American Man Hug (Figure 2.6)

Some men in America are not even completely comfortable with the fully embracing style of hugging, even when done correctly. For men who cannot quite bring themselves to use both arms in the hug, the American Man Hug is an appropriate compromise.

FIGURE 2.6 The American Man Hug.

1. Begin with a traditional firm handshake
2. Keeping your hand clasped with your buddy, wrap the left arm around the shoulder of your friend.
3. Slap your friend's back two times. As in the international style, the back slap is key.
4. Release embrace.

BEYOND G-STRINGS AND KEG STANDS: ◄ THROWING A CLASSY BACHELOR PARTY ►

One of the great traditions of male friendship is the holding of a bachelor party before a buddy gets hitched. Done right, the bachelor party can serve as a memorable weigh station in a man's important rite of passage from single dude to manly husband.

THE HISTORY OF THE BACHELOR PARTY

Men may be surprised to learn that the tradition of having a bachelor party is rooted in ancient times. The Spartans, who originated the idea in the fifth century B.C., would hold a dinner for the groom-to-be on the night before his wedding. The evening would be spent feasting and toasting the groom and each other.

The tradition of having a "bachelor's dinner" continued into modern times. In the 1940s and 1950s the occasion was called a "gentlemen's dinner." It was thrown by the groom's father and involved the same toasting and eating that the Spartans had enjoyed. These bachelor dinners were designed for male bonding and to celebrate the groom-to-be's important rite of passage from single life to marriage.

Some time during the last few decades, the dinner was dropped and a party took its place. Breaking bread and toasting were exchanged for, or supplemented with, strippers, gambling and copious amounts of alcohol.

Fortunately these kinds of parties have been going out of style of late. Such parties neither honor the bride-to-be, who will be stressed by the temptations her fiancé may succumb to, nor respect your friend, who has likely reached a point of maturity in which he feels ready to get married and settle down. So instead of viewing a bachelor party as your friend's last chance for debauchery, a party should really serve as a golden opportunity for male bonding, a chance to do activities that may become less frequent post-marriage and a time to blow off any prenuptial jitters.

PLANNING AND EXECUTING A GENTLEMANLY BACHELOR'S PARTY

If you are selected to be your friend's best man in his wedding, the job of planning this ancient tradition rests on your shoulders. Following these steps will ensure that you honor your best friend with a bachelor's party that is both classy and enjoyable.

Pick an Activity

The first step in planning a bachelor party is to choose an activity to center the party around. Just because your fiesta won't involve stuffing dollar bills into G-strings doesn't mean you can't get your JOLLIFICATION on. There are plenty of other activities that will unleash your testosterone and get your heart pumping. Here are just a few ideas:

- Rent Jet Skis for a day on the water
- Go snow skiing or snowboarding
- Attend a professional or collegiate sporting event
- Attend a boxing or mixed martial arts match
- Spend the day golfing (FIGURE 2.7)
- Take a deep-sea fishing trip, charter a fishing boat or take a lesson in fly-fishing

FIGURE 2.7 The first step in planning a bachelor party is to choose an activity to center the party around. For example, you could spend the day golfing.

- Plan a game of a football, basketball, soccer or bowling
- Play a poker tournament
- Go play paintball
- Take a camping or backpacking trip

As you're choosing an activity, keep these tips in mind:

- Don't do anything insanely dangerous. You want to have fun, but you don't want to risk breaking one of the groom's limbs. He'll find it difficult to go scuba diving on his honeymoon with a cast on his leg.
- It's nice to surprise your friend with what he'll be doing at his party, but be sure to cater to his personality and interests.
- Consider the relative budgets of your friends. You don't want some of the groom's friends to skip the party because they can't afford to come.

- After you choose an activity for the bachelor's party, plan for a meal to follow it. If the weather is warm, a backyard cookout makes an excellent choice. If it's cooler, or you simply desire something more formal, rent a room at your friend's favorite restaurant.
- At the dinner, encourage your friends to make funny roasts and poignant toasts. They may also wish to impart words of wisdom to the groom. If you have some advice or want to say things that won't be included in your best man speech, contribute to the toasting.

Choose a Date

There are several considerations to take into account when planning the date of the party. While it is tempting to have the party the night before the wedding when all the guests are in town, this is not an appropriate choice. The groom needs to be sharp for the next day's ceremony, not all tuckered out. Also, a rehearsal dinner is often planned for the same night and would conflict with your party. So choose a date several weeks before the wedding. If many of the groom's friends live out-of-state, you may want to push it back even further, so they need not make the same trip twice in a short period of time.

Send Out the Invitations

Invite all the men in the wedding party and all of the groom's good friends and male relatives with whom he is close. Traditionally it is considered impolite to invite people to prewedding functions that are not invited to the wedding itself. Yet this rule has always been applied more ambiguously when it comes to bachelor parties. If the groom is having a very small wedding or a destination wedding, it may be appropriate to invite friends who are not invited to the main event. Consult with the groom as you compile the guest list.

Send out the invitations about three weeks before the party. The invitations should match the party's level of formality. If the party is to be formal, send quality handwritten invitations through the mail. If the party is going to be a more casual affair, a phone call or e-mail will do. If the party will involve an activity such as the ones mentioned above, include information such as the cost, meeting place and time, maps, etc.

Each invitee should be responsible for paying for the cost of himself and chipping into the cost for the groom. In the invitation, include a respectful request for a check to be sent to you for the appropriate amount.

GIVE A BEST MAN SPEECH THAT WON'T MAKE PEOPLE CRINGE

At some point in your life, one of your buddies or your brother will probably ask you to be the best man in his wedding. This is a great honor. One of the duties of a best man is to give a speech wherein you say a few kind words about your friend/brother and his new wife. If you've been to many weddings, you know that oftentimes best man speeches can quickly devolve into an awkward, drunken spectacle. The mixture of booze and lack of preparation results in the best man rambling and sharing inappropriate and embarrassing stories about the groom in front of hundreds of family and friends.

If you don't want to make yourself look like a CLASSICAL IGNORAMUS and you want to truly be the best man, here are a few pointers to keep in mind as you prepare to give your speech:

Prepare. Don't walk into the wedding reception thinking you'll know exactly what to say when you get there. If you have a few months before the wedding, start mulling over some ideas for the speech. Begin brainstorming and jotting down thoughts, stories, jokes and quotes you might want to use. If you don't know a lot about how your buddy and his wife met, ask. Think of stories from you and your buddy's past that show what a great guy he is. The goal of the speech is to celebrate the couple and make them look good.

Stay sober. Sure, you want to enjoy yourself, and yes, alcohol may help take the edge off of giving a speech in front of hundreds of strangers, but make sure you're not sloppy drunk when you give your speech. You don't want to be completely uninhibited or you might say something you'll regret later on. Besides, a real man doesn't need a crutch to help him tackle a challenge. Be man enough to postpone your own gratification until after the speech is completed.

Tell a story that makes a connection. The ideal way to structure a best man speech is to find a connection between a story about your friend and your support for the couple. Share a story about how your friend would always lament that he would never find a woman with x,y and z qualities, but how he finally did in his new bride. Or tell a story about the moment when you were hanging out with the couple and you realized your friend had found his match. Another good angle is to talk about the way that

FIGURE 2.8 Avoid controversial, offensive or embarrassing topics in your best man speech.

the bride and groom balance one another. Relate a funny (not embarrassing, see below) anecdote in which one of your buddy's personality traits tripped him up in some way. For example, the story could be about how your friend is very shy and how this shyness caused some humorous event to occur. You then talk about how bubbly and outgoing his bride is, and how they therefore make a perfect team.

Avoid controversial, offensive or embarrassing topics. You would think this is common sense, but people somehow forget this when they're standing with a microphone in their hand in front of a crowd of people. What gets people in trouble is attempting to be funny by sharing an embarrassing story or cracking some lame joke about a ball and chain. Such shtick usually bombs. It's okay to share a humorous anecdote, but not one that gets laughs at the expense of your friend and his new wife and embarrasses them and their guests. **(FIGURE 2.8)**

Avoid inside jokes. If you want to keep people's attention, save the inside jokes for when it's just you and your friend.

Keep it short. Nothing irritates people more than some rambling drunk going on and on and on. People have probably already listened to the maid of honor and the bride's father give their spiel. By the time they get to you, the crowd is ready to eat cake and get on with it. Shoot for no more than five minutes.

Other don'ts. Don't talk about the groom's past relationships, don't tell people what you really thought of your buddy's wife when you first met her, don't slam the food, don't make comments about looking forward to the honeymoon while winking at the bride—basically just use some tact and class.

Remember to be yourself. No need to get formal or try to be someone you're not. And there's no need to follow these instructions exactly either. Simply use them as a guide and be yourself. Let it flow naturally.

Use your natural voice and mannerisms. Make it personal and sincere and say things from the heart and you should be golden.

MANLY ADVICE

BEST MAN
SPEECH CRIB SHEET

1. Open by thanking those who made the day possible. Single out the bride and groom's parents by name, and offer a toast to them for not only putting on the wedding but for raising two fine people. Thank the guests for coming.

2. Transition to your speech: "I am especially glad to be here on this occasion to celebrate this wonderful day with my friend/brother."

3. Talk about how you know the groom, why you're grateful for having him as your friend and why he's such an upstanding guy.

4. Share a story about your friend and connect it to the couple.

5. Raise your glass and say something to the effect of: "Here's to a lifetime of happiness and love for _____ and _____!"

6. Let out a sigh of relief.

CHAPTER THREE

THE HERO

"The difference between a hero
and a coward is one step sideways."
—GENE HACKMAN

As little boys, we all dreamed of growing up to be just like the super-heroes in comic books. We wanted to have the supercool gadgets, the sweet costume and the extraordinary powers necessary to swoop in and save the day. Somewhere along the way, whether the epiphany came when jumping from a roof with only a sheet cape for wings, or waiting in vain for that spider bite to develop into something more than an itchy bump, we grew up and realized that we were never going to be the next Superman or develop Spidey sense.

But every man, even sans tights, can be a hero. The annals of history are filled with tales of ordinary men who risked their own lives to save others. In our time, we have stories of well-known heroes like Todd Beamer and his plan to overthrow the terrorists of Flight 93, and Wesley Autrey who covered himself over a seizure victim to protect him from an oncoming subway train. And every local community has lesser-known tales like that of William Kirby, who broke down the door of his neighbor's burning house to save her. Everyone loves to hear of such heroic acts not only because they are inspiring but because they are rarer in an increasingly anonymous and isolated society, a world where it is far easier to step over the man in need than to risk life and limb to save him.

Yet sacrifice is one of the key qualities of true men. Every man must be ready to put aside thoughts of his own welfare or pressing schedule and be willing to come to the aid of those in need. No man knows precisely how he will act in the moment of crisis. But he can prepare himself to make the right choice when that day comes by daily cultivating a generous and compassionate attitude and by learning the skills necessary to be able to step in to help without hesitation. The chaos of an emergency is not the time to figure out how to proceed, you must learn now the knowledge needed to become a real hero.

"I always believe in being prepared, even when I'm dressed in white tie and tails."

—GEORGE S. PATTON JR.

Let's say you're out with your buddies (or maybe a lovely young lady) having a good time, when all of a sudden some THOROUGH-PACED SCOUNDREL shoves you. You didn't do anything to instigate the guy, but it doesn't matter. There is a special breed of males, that when inebriated, start fights with random people. This breed, when found in their wild habitat, are often accompanied by their similarly boneheaded buddies.

Or perhaps you and your posse end up in a rumble with the Socs because one of your buddies killed a Soc while trying to save Ponyboy from being drowned by some punk Soc. Man, I hate them Socs.

What should you do in these situations? If possible, it's best to follow the advice given to Ponyboy and stay golden. Always try to avoid the fight altogether. Attempt to defuse the situation by talking with the guy. Try to get him to calm down. If you did something to unknowingly RAISE HIS BRISTLES (like looking at him funny), then apologize. Don't let your ego get in the way of apologizing for something you didn't do.

If talking to the knucklehead doesn't work, start to leave the scene. But maintain alertness and walk away backwards, still facing your opponent. If he's a no-good yellow-belly rat, he'll attack you from behind.

If the ruffian is still threatening you and you have nowhere to go, then it's time to get down to business. You could pull out some tried-and-true street-fighting moves and go in for the head butt or start brandishing a broken bottle. But now that you're donning a hat and dressing like a gentleman, you might as well learn how to fight like one. For that, we must turn back the hands of time, walk the rough and tumble streets of nineteenth-century London and enter the hallowed halls of the Bartitsu Club.

THE HISTORY
OF BARTITSU

Before Randy Couture and the Ultimate Fighting Championship, there was Edward William Barton-Wright and bartitsu. Born at the turn of the century, bartitsu was probably the first instance of what we know today as mixed martial arts. Mr. Barton, an English railroad conductor turned martial arts instructor, combined elements of boxing, jujitsu, cane fighting and French kickboxing to create a self-defense system that could be used by discerning gentlemen on the mean streets of Edwardian London. Bartitsu grew to such popularity that even Sherlock Holmes was employing it on his sleuthing adventures.

Barton taught bartitsu until the 1920s when its popularity and practice waned and then disappeared almost completely. Yet the legacy Barton left behind was a system of techniques and moves that can still foil the plans of pernicious scamps and scallywags that come your way.

THE MARTIAL ARTS OF BARTITSU

Bartitsu was a mix of several different marital arts. Each added distinct tactics that made bartitsu a versatile system for defending oneself and taking on an attacker. Below is a brief description of each.

Boxing

The boxing style implemented by Barton was the style used by golden age fisticuffers of the time. Unlike the modern style, boxers during the nineteenth and early twentieth centuries maintained a stiff and upright stance. Usually the lead hand was extended, with the rear forearm "barring the mark," or covering their chest area.

Jujitsu

Bartitsu borrowed half of its name and many of its moves from the Japanese fighting style of jujitsu. During the late nineteenth century, jujitsu had become a popular sport among Westerners. In fact, President Teddy Roosevelt was a practitioner of this martial art. Barton brought in famous Japanese jujitsu instructors or jujutsukas K. Tani, S. Yamamonto and Yukio Tani to teach at his school, the Bartitsu Club. In a March 1899 issue of *Pearson's Magazine*, Barton summarized jujitsu in three principles:

1. To disturb the equilibrium of your assailant.
2. To surprise him before he has time to regain his balance and use his strength.
3. If necessary to subject the joints of any parts of his body, whether neck, shoulder, elbow, wrist, back, knee, ankle, etc., to strains that they are anatomically and mechanically unable to resist.

La Savate

La savate (pronounced *savat*) is a French kickboxing system developed from street-fighting sailors in the port of Marseilles during the nineteenth century. Sailors in Marseilles had to develop a way to fight that didn't involve closed fists because they were considered deadly weapons and carried legal penalties if used. Thus, savate consisted of different kicks, openhanded slaps and grappling.

Stick Fighting

Also known as "la canne," stick fighting was another French martial art. Barton brought in Pierre Vigny, a Swiss master-at-arms, to teach

FIGURE 3.1 Because many upper-class Englishmen carried canes and umbrellas, Vigny modified the traditional form of stick fighting to better implement these instruments.

stick fighting. Because many upper-class Englishmen carried canes and umbrellas, Vigny modified the traditional form of stick fighting to better implement these instruments. His system was simple and efficient, and it lent itself to defending oneself in an altercation in the streets. Strikes to the face, head, neck, wrists, knees and shins were used to eliminate the threat of an attacker. **(FIGURE 3.1)**

Using Bartitsu in a Street Fight

"The unforgivable crime is soft hitting. Do not hit at all if it can be avoided; but never hit softly."

—THEODORE ROOSEVELT

If you've been accosted by some RANK SPOON, and they're not backing down, it's time to put up your dukes and fight. Start by assuming a stable fighting stance. Spread your stance to about shoulder width apart and slightly bend your knees. The goal is to maintain balance so you don't end up on the ground. Keep your hands up to protect your face and clench your teeth. A solid punch to an open mouth can lead to a broken jaw. From here you are ready to go all Sherlock Holmes on this CHUCKLEHEAD.

Offensive Bartitsu Moves

Here's how to perform some of the most effective moves Barton took from the marital arts above and incorporated into Bartitsu.

BASIC BOXING TECHNIQUES

The jab. While it's not the most powerful punch, the jab is an important tool in your boxing arsenal. It's used primarily to wear your opponent down and to open him up for the power punch. The jab is performed with your lead hand by quickly extending your arm. Twist your arm in a corkscrew like motion just before impact. The twist will give your jab some added oomph. **(FIGURE 3.2)**

The hook. Like the hook, the jab is performed with your lead hand. Unlike the jab, the power from the hook is coming from your core, not

FIGURE 3.2 The jab is used primarily to wear your opponent down and to open him up for the power punch.

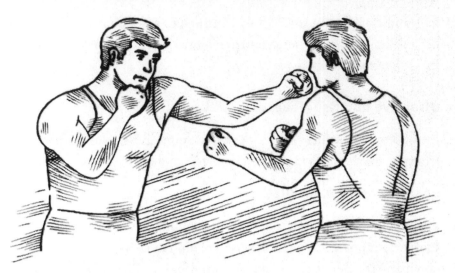

FIGURE 3.3 If done correctly, a well-placed hook can knock out an opponent.

your arm. Bend your lead arm, as if you're holding a shield. Pivot your front foot, like your squishing a bug. At the same time, twist your torso. Aim your fist at your opponent's chin. If done correctly, a well-placed hook can knock out an opponent. **(FIGURE 3.3)**

The overhand punch. You'll have to do some work to open up your opponent so you can land this SOCKDOLOGER. Try some high jabs to the head and a few fakes. When your opponent drops his guard, you're ready to throw your power punch. End with a jab from your nondominant hand so that your dominant hand is ready to throw the overhand punch.

Bring your jab back while simultaneously throwing your overhand punch. Increase the power of your punch by pushing off your back foot and twisting your hips much like you would swing a baseball bat. Don't aim at his face, but rather a couple of inches behind his face. That way you'll have maximum power when your fist lands on your opponent's ugly mug. A well-executed overhand punch will leave your opponent CATAWAMPTIOUSLY CHEWED UP.

Overhand punches do leave you vulnerable after you throw them, however. So keep your jab hand up by your face to protect against any

FIGURE 3.4 A well-executed overhand punch will leave your opponent beaten and destroyed.

counters. Spinning away from your opponent after you throw the punch can also create distance between you and him. **(FIGURE 3.4)**

BASIC JUJITSU TECHNIQUES

Shoulder lock. If your opponent throws a punch at you, step back and deflect the strike with a downward block. Quickly strike your opponent with your right palm in his right shoulder. With your right hand now on your opponent's shoulder, pull it down while you place your left arm under his right arm. Now put your left hand on top of your right hand. Your opponent should now be doubled over with their right arm resting on your left shoulder. In this position, strike your opponent in the face with a knee.

Sweeping ankle throw. This move will take your opponent's feet out from under him. Grab your attacker by the coat lapels. If he's not wearing a coat, grab his shirt where the lapels would be. Pull him forward quickly while sweeping your right foot into his left foot. If done correctly, this should take your opponent to the ground where you can establish more control.

BASIC CANE FIGHTING TECHNIQUES

The jab. The jab can be performed with either the point or the butt of the cane. Using the point is more effective and will cause greater pain. Perform the jab by quickly stabbing your opponent and retracting your hand quickly. The quickness of the jab makes it a difficult move to defend.

The thrust. The thrust is similar to the jab in that you use a stabbing motion. It differs from the jab because it's delivered over a longer distance and requires full extension of the arm. Standing in an attack position, quickly lunge forward and extend the tip of the cane toward your attacker. For added oomph, put as much of your body weight behind the thrust as you can.

Cuts. Cuts can be performed either high or low, in up, down, right or left directions. A cut is performed with a chopping motion. Down-

FIGURE 3.5 The coup de pied bas is a sweeping kick aimed at the lower legs of an opponent.

ward cuts are probably the strongest motion and are also the most difficult to defend.

BASIC SAVATE TECHNIQUES

Chasse crossie kicks. A chasse lateral kick is performed by crossing the rear foot behind the lead and then lifting the knee of the kicking foot toward the opposite shoulder. Add a hop before you strike. You can then strike with your foot aiming for the head, torso or thighs of an opponent.

Coup de pied bas. This is a sweeping kick aimed at the lower legs of an opponent. The kick is performed by pivoting the kicking foot from the hip. Your leg remains fully extended. You can either try to sweep an opponent off his feet or simply aim for his knees or ankles to inflict some pain. **(FIGURE 3.5)**

Defensive Bartitsu Moves

Barton also included some creative and effective self-defense techniques that used improvised weapons and surprises and were well-suited to the gentleman fighter.

USING A CLOAK OR OVERCOAT TO DEFEND YOURSELF

Using your cloak or overcoat is an effective defensive tool, even when an attacker is brandishing a knife. While walking in the street, wear your overcoat draped over your shoulders without passing your arms through the sleeves. If your assailant attacks, take your right hand and grab the left collar of your coat and, in one sweeping motion, shroud your opponents head with the coat. Your attacker will be surprised and momentarily blind, which gives you plenty of time to punch him in the gut or give him several licks to the head. **(FIGURE 3.6)**

You can also choose to slip behind your opponent while you have the coat over his head, grab his ankle with your left hand and simultaneously push his back so that he falls forward on his face. From here you

FIGURE 3.6 If your assailant attacks, take your right hand and grab the left collar of your coat and, in one sweeping motion, shroud your opponents head with the coat.

FIGURE 3.7 Slip behind your opponent while you have the coat over his head, grab his ankle with your left hand and simultaneously push his back so that he falls forward on his face.

CHAPTER THREE

can put your opponent in an appropriate jujitsu hold until the police come. **(FIGURE 3.7)**

USING A HAT TO DEFEND YOURSELF

A hat can also be used to distract or temporarily blind an attacker. When an attacker gets near you, take off your hat with a sweeping motion and burrow your opponents face into it. Either wallop him in the gut or take him down to the ground to put him in a submission hold.

A hat can also be used as a shield to defend yourself from punches or attacks from knives. Grasping the hat firmly by the brim in your left hand, hold the hat away from your body to the side. If an attacker makes a thrust at you with a knife, catch the blow with your hat and deliver a blow to the attacker's face with your free hand.

◀ BREAK DOWN A DOOR ▶

You're in a burning house and you need to escape and the door is on fire. Or your loved ones are in a burning house and you're locked out. Or perhaps a loved one is stricken with a medical emergency and is locked inside a room or in their house. What to do? Be a man, dammit! Break down that door! You know you've always wanted to.

If you have watched enough movies, your next move is a no-brainer ... run at the door shoulder first, right? Wrong. This technique may be uber-manly, but it will probably dislocate your shoulder. It's better to employ a more forceful and well-placed kick.

Find which way the door opens by checking the hinges. Kicking a door down is best employed on a door that swings away from you. If the door opens towards you, you might as well be MILKING THE PIGEON.

Kick to the side of where the lock is mounted (near the keyhole). This is typically the weakest part of the door.

Using a front kick, drive the heel of your foot into the door. Give the kick forward momentum and keep your balance by driving the heel of your standing foot into the ground. Don't kick the lock itself; this could break your foot.

The wood should begin to splinter. Today many doors are made of soft wood and are hollow. They should give way fairly easily, especially since a deadlock bolt extends only an inch or less into the door frame. Older completely solid doors will prove more resistant. Just keep on kicking until the door gives way and you can save the day.

Avoid jump kicks. While you may be tempted to employ this manly move, jumping, even if preceded by "the crane," diminishes your stability which causes you to lose power.

◀ PERFORM THE FIREMAN'S CARRY ▶

"A hero is a man who does what he can."

—ROMAIN ROLLAND

The fireman's carry is hands-down the manliest way of carrying a person to safety. And it not only looks awesome, it's actually an effective way to distribute someone's weight, allowing you to haul them over long distances with minimal strain. **(FIGURE 3.8)**

1. Raise the victim to a standing position. This is no easy task when they're dead to the world. Start by rolling them on their stomach and kneel by their head. Stick your arms under their armpits and around their back. Raise the victim to his feet. Lift with your legs, not with your back.

2. Shift your weight to your right leg and stick it between the victim's legs. Grab the victim's right hand with your left, and drape it over your shoulder. With your head under the victim's right armpit, wrap your arm around the back of his right knee. Squat down and position his body on your shoulders. Try to equally distribute his body weight on each side.

3. Grab the victim's right hand with your right hand. Your left hand is free to judo chop would-be assailants.

4. Transport your victim.

FIGURE 3.8 The fireman's carry is an effective way to distribute someone's weight, allowing you to haul them over long distances with minimal strain.

◄ SAVE A DROWNING PERSON ►

You're at the lake with your friends and family. You're grilling some tasty man burgers and taking in the beautiful sunny day. As you gaze over the water, you see a man thrashing his arms around and gasping for air. It's time to get your David Hasselhoff on and save this drowning person. Your golden brown hairy chest was made for a moment like this. You start to run towards the lake.

Unfortunately, since you're at the lake and not the ocean, your fantasy of being the Hoff ends here. Contrary to what you see on television and in movies, your best move is not to dash into the water after the person. Drowning people aren't only a danger to themselves; they're a danger to the people rescuing them, too. Panicked and flailing about, they can pull and push you under when you try to help.

If the person is near the shore or you're in a boat, try these two methods first:

1. Pull the person to safety with a stick. Grab a long tree limb or pole and extend it out to the victim. Tell them to grab on. Pull them to safety.

2. Throw an object out to them attached to a rope. If you're near a body of water, it's always good to have a safety ring close by. If you don't have one, improvise by tying a rope to an object and throwing it out to the person. **(FIGURE 3.9)**

FIGURE 3.9 Save a drowning person by throwing an object out to them attached to a rope.

If the person is too far away to rescue with either of these methods, you'll need to get in the water to save them. When rescuing a person from the water, take these precautions to avoid getting drowned yourself.

1. Calm the person down. As you approach the person, talk to them and let them know that everything is going to be fine. It makes getting them out of the water much easier.

2. If you have a floatation device and the victim is simply too far off for you to throw it from shore, swim out close enough to be able to toss it to them. If the floating object is tethered to a rope, pull them to shore. If not, simply have them grab on.

3. Approach the person from the back. You want to be out of the reach of the victim's arms and legs. As mentioned above, your victim will probably try to grab on to you and thus will pull you down to the murky depths. So approach the person from behind and wrap your arm around his chest. Keep his head above the water.

4. If the victim does try to pull you down, ignore your instinct to fight it and instead sink and/or swim downward on purpose. The victim's primal instinct to stay above water will kick in, and he'll release you.

5. Swim back to safety. Using your free arm, swim back to safety. Tell your victim to stay calm and float on his back.

◀ TREAT A SNAKEBITE ▶

You and your buddies are on a camping trip reconnecting with nature and your masculinity. You're taking a day hike to see some ancient Indian hieroglyphs, when your friend cries out in pain as two razor sharp fangs sink into his ankle. He's just been bitten by a snake. Do you know what to do?

You better. Getting bitten by a venomous snake is serious business. While the reactions vary from snake to snake, all venom is essentially designed to immobilize the victim and start the process of digestion. Venom is basically toxic snake saliva, ready to turn your friend into dinner. Seek medical attention immediately, even if you don't think the snake is poisonous. Here's what to do while you wait for medics to arrive or if you're in a remote locale, far from civilization.

The Dos

Do wash the bite with soap and water as soon as possible. You want to remove as much of the snake's spit as you can.

Do keep the bitten area below the victim's heart. This is done to slow the flow of the venom.

Do take off any rings or watches. The venom is going to make your friend swell and jewelry might cut off his circulation.

Do tightly wrap a bandage 2 to 4 inches above the bite. If you can't reach medical care within thirty minutes, wrap a bandage around the bitten appendage. This is to assist in reducing the flow of venom. You want to make it tight, but not too tight as to completely cut off the appendage's circulation. That will only cause tissue damage.

Do try to draw the venom out of the wound. If you have a snake bite kit, place the suction device over the bite to help draw the venom out. Leave on for a maximum of ten minutes. If used properly, a suction device can remove up to 30 percent of the venom.

The Don'ts

Don't cut the wound. While watching an old Western, you might have seen a cowboy making an incision above the snakebite in order to "drain" the venom. This isn't a smart move because you increase the chances of infection in the area.

Don't suck the venom. Another remedy we all have seen in the movies is people sucking out the venom with their mouth. You don't want the venom in your mouth where it can get into your bloodstream.

Don't apply ice to the wound. Ice can cause tissue and skin damage and inhibits the removal of venom when using a suction device.

Don't panic. Try to keep your friend from freaking out. The more he moves and the faster his hearts beats, the quicker the venom is going to circulate through his body. So keep your buddy still and tell him the story of the time you stole your rival high school's mascot and held it captive for a week.

◄ BE A HERO ON THE ROAD ►

"A boy doesn't have to go to war to be a hero; he can say he doesn't like pie when he sees there isn't enough to go around."

—EDGAR WATSON HOWE

It's a familiar sight to anyone who has traveled this nation's highways and byways: the desperate motorist stranded at the side of the road without either the proper tools or the necessary knowledge to fix their car's malfunction. Will you drive on by because you also lack these things? Or will you play the role of the Good Samaritan and stop to help them on their way? Every man should know how to confidently perform two basic car repairs: jump-starting a car and changing a flat tire. Such acts may not be as dramatic as leaping tall buildings in a single bound, but you can bet someone will always be grateful you swooped in to save them.

How to Change a Flat Tire

Tools needed: Spare tire, jack, lug wrench.

1. Park the car on a flat surface. Be sure to put on the emergency brake. It's also recommended to put a block on the tire opposite of the flat tire. Here's a blocking example: If the right rear tire is flat, put the block on the front left tire.

2. Remove the hubcap. If the car has a hubcap, remove it so you can get to the lug nuts. Use the hubcap to hold the nuts, just like the dad in *A Christmas Story*. Just don't let your kid hold the hubcap or he'll lose the nuts and drop the F-bomb.

3. Loosen the nuts. Grab your lug wrench and place it on the flat tire's lug nuts. Loosen them up by turning them counterclock-

FIGURE 3.10 Loosen the lug nuts up by turning them counterclockwise. Loosen the nuts a few turns, but don't take any of them off yet!

wise. The nuts are probably on there really tight, so you'll have to use all your man strength to unscrew them. Loosen the nuts a few turns, but don't take any of them off yet! **(FIGURE 3.10)**

4. Place the jack underneath the car. Check the owner's manual for the correct placement of the jack. Turn the hand crank at the end of the jack to raise the jack until it comes into contact with the car's frame. Make sure it's touching a sturdy spot.

5. Jack it up! Start cranking the jack until the wheel is high enough above the ground to remove the tire.

6. Remove the flat. Remove the lug nuts from the wheel. You should be able to do it by hand because you've already loosened them. Remove the flat tire and lay it flat. You don't want the wheel to roll into traffic during rush hour and cause a thirty car pileup.

7. Slap on the spare. Take your spare tire and line up the lugs, or bolts, with the holes in the wheel and slide the wheel on. Once the wheel is on, take your lug nuts and tighten them by hand until you meet firm resistance.

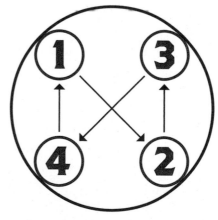

FIGURE 3.11 Use this tightening pattern if you have five bolts on your wheel.

FIGURE 3.12 If your car has four bolts on the wheel, use this pattern

8. Lower the car. Lower the jack until the wheel is firmly on the ground.

9. Finish tightening the lug nuts. These babies must be on super tight so the wheel doesn't come flying off while driving to the tire shop to get the flat fixed. So you need to unleash the superpower of the star pattern to get those lugs on tighter than a deer tick. Start with any lug nut, then follow this pattern. **(FIGURES 3.11, 3.12)**

10. Get the person off to a tire shop. Spare tires aren't supposed to be driven on for long distances, so they'll need to get their flat tire fixed and replaced as soon as possible.

How to Jump-Start a Car With Cables

Tools needed: Another car, jumper cables.

1. Make sure both cars are turned off.

2. Connect one end of the red (positive) jumper cable to the positive terminal on the stalled battery.

3. Then connect the other red (positive) cable clamp to the positive terminal of the good battery.

4. Connect one end of the black (negative) jumper cable to the negative terminal of the good battery.

5. Then connect the other black (negative) cable to a clean, unpainted metal surface under the disabled car's hood. Somewhere on the engine block is a good place. Unless you want to see flying sparks and a possible explosion, do not connect the negative cable to the negative terminal of the dead battery.

6. Start the car that's doing the jumping and allow it to run for about two to three minutes before starting the dead car.

7. Remove cables in reverse order of how you connected them.

8. Keep the jumped car running for at least thirty minutes to give the battery sufficient time to recharge itself.

9. Give yourself a pat on the back for a manly job well done.

How to Jump-Start a Car Without Cables

If the car has a standard transmission, you can jump-start that bad boy without using cables. Here's how you do it.

Tools Needed: Elbow grease, a hill or compliant friends.

1. Find a stretch of downhill road that's clear.

2. Fully depress the clutch and put the car in second gear.

3. Turn the ignition to the on position.

4. Take your foot off the brake and start rolling down the hill, keeping the clutch fully depressed.

5. Coast down the hill until you reach 5 to 7 miles per hour.

6. Release the clutch quickly. You should feel the engine turn and start. If it doesn't start the first time, depress the clutch and release it again.

7. If you don't have a hill, get some of your buddies to help push and follow the steps above.

MAYDAY! MAYDAY!
◄ LAND A PLANE IN AN EMERGENCY ►

"Self-trust is the essence of heroism."

—RALPH WALDO EMERSON

We've all had the thought cross our mind while flying, "What if the pilot(s) somehow became incapacitated and I had to land this thing? What would I do?" Or maybe more timely for today's world, "What if a terrorist takes over the plane, and I have to save the day by knocking him out with a Chuck Norris-style thump to the head?"

You're a hero, boo-yah! But if the pilot's unconscious, you may have to get the plane on the ground. Relax, it's not as hard as it looks, and if you follow a few simple steps, you'll be on the ground safely and in one piece for your press conference and hero shots.

Maintain Aircraft Control (Straight and Level)

When you first arrive in the cockpit, take the left seat if possible. This is generally where the captain or aircraft commander sits, and it often has easier access to some of the instruments you'll need to fly. However, the majority of dual seat aircraft can be flown from either side.

As soon as you sit down, take a deep breath and look outside to see if the aircraft is in a dive, climb, turn, etc. If it appears to be straight and level, then don't touch the flight controls; the autopilot is most likely on and there's no need to interfere. If, however, the airplane is racing towards the ground or in a steep turn, you need to use the stick or yoke (pilot speak for steering wheel) to bring it back to level flight. Just like in the video games, you pull back on the yoke to make it climb, push forward to make it descend, and move it right or left to turn.

If you are in the clouds and can't tell the attitude of the aircraft, it will be necessary to use the altitude indicator, also referred to as the artificial horizon. This is an instrument that gives a representation of the aircraft in relation to the ground and sky. If you're on a jet of some sort, chances are high that it will be displayed on the screen directly in front of you. The *W* shape in the middle represents the wings of the aircraft, the brown represents ground and the blue represents sky. So if you see half brown, half blue it means you are in level flight, which is what you want. If you see anything else, make corrections with the stick as necessary to line up the wings of the aircraft with the horizon line.

MAKE A RADIO CALL

After you have the aircraft under control, the next step is to contact Air Traffic Control (ATC) over the radio to explain the situation and ask for help. The majority of aircraft have a radio mic switch on the yoke on the back where your index finger would rest when you grasped it normally. The problem is that the autopilot disconnect switch is often placed on the yoke as well and without proper knowledge of the autopilot system, an inadvertent disconnect of the autopilot could result in a major disaster. A safer alternative is using the handheld radio normally mounted

FIGURE 3.13 Try making a call on the radio frequency currently selected and see if you get a response. Say "Mayday" and state who you are and what has happened.

to the left of the pilot's seat just below the side window. Use it just like you would use a CB radio: Push to talk and release to listen.

Try making a call on the radio frequency currently selected and see if you get a response. Say "Mayday" and state who you are and what has happened. Don't worry about radio etiquette; it's an emergency, so just use plain English and tell them you don't know what you're doing and need some help. Don't sound too panicked. You're a man after all and completely in control of the situation. **(FIGURE 3.13)**

After talking, remember to release the mic button to listen. If no one responds, try changing the VHF radio frequency to 121.5 MHz (this is known as "Guard" and is monitored by everyone). The radio unit will normally be located on the center pedestal in between the pilot's and copilot's seats or directly in front of you on the center panel.

Do What They Tell You

Just like in the movies, what happens next is various agencies will be notified of your emergency and experts will walk you through getting the plane on the ground. They'll know the cockpit layout and be able to tell you where a button or switch is located and what you need to do with it. They'll also be working in conjunction with ATC to navigate you to an airport where you will be able to land. As long as you follow their instructions to the letter, everything should turn out just fine. You may not have the prettiest landing, but you'll survive.

Get It on the Ground

While many of today's jets are fully automated, they can't quite land themselves. But thankfully for you, they do have the capability to get you lined up on the runway's center line on a proper glide path so that you can take over at 50-100 feet off the ground. All you will have to do manually is:

1. Flare (pull up slightly on the stick just prior to touchdown so the main gear hit first)
2. Fly the nosewheel to the ground (push the stick forward until the front touches down)
3. Pull the throttles all the way back
4. Step on the brakes which are located on the tops of the rudder pedals down by your feet.

If you find yourself veering off the runway, lightly step on the rudder pedals to steer yourself back to centerline.

You've landed! It's incredible; you're now the hero of the day! Next stop: ticker tape parade.

CHAPTER FOUR

◂‖THE‖▸
LOVER

"He is not a lover
who does not love forever."
—EURIPIDES

I t used to be that a man worked hard to be worthy of a woman's love. Instead of being mere sexual objects, women were seen as people who deserved the very best from a man. Men would direct all their sexual passions to becoming the best man they could be so they could win the heart of the woman they loved. During medieval times, knights lived by the code of chivalry, roaming the countryside and gallantly protecting and winning the hearts of damsels in distress. In the Victorian era, men sought to win the affections of ladies through elaborate rituals of calling cards, parlor visits, balls and buggy rides. When men went off to fight the Big One, the memory of a beautiful dame back home carried them through many a long and dark night in the belly of a submarine. In the 1950s, a man asked his favorite girl to go steady and proved his affections by pinning her with his fraternity badge.

Fast-forward to the modern day. Women no longer want to be rescued by a man, "hanging out" has supplanted dating and "going steady" has been resigned to the dust pile of embarrassing terms alongside "necking and petting." Of course, one shouldn't look to the past through the glasses of uncritical nostalgia. History may be filled with golden examples of romantic love, but it was also marked by the assumption of a woman's inferiority. Yet in our attempt to completely equalize the relations between the sexes, the art of gentlemanly court-ship was thrown out with the bathwater.

Ask any woman today what her biggest complaint is about men and she'll probably tell you that there aren't any real men to be found. What they see are a bunch of boys walking around in men's bodies. But they're looking for a man who will take care of them, a man who knows how to treat a lady. They're looking for men who take initiative in a relationship and are willing to commit.

Unfortunately for women, these manly qualities are in short supply. Men have forgotten the art of romance and the responsibilities of love. Under the guise of equality, they've stopped working for a woman's love altogether. They want the benefits of relationships without any of the responsibilities.

A woman can still be a man's equal, and yet be worthy of being treated with honor, respect and swoon-worthy romance. Relationships should still involve affectionate courting, romantic traditions and a little mystery. Sure, this may sound old-fashioned and quaint. But with all the ills that plague modern relationships, perhaps we can take a lesson from our forebears. Reading the letters and hearing the stories of our grandparents reveals how happy they were together and how much affection they had for one another. Perhaps we, too, can experience the happiness and joy that comes with being a gentlemanly lover.

◄ THE ART OF CHIVALRY ►

"The motto of chivalry is also the motto of wisdom; to serve all, but love only one."

—HONORE DE BALZAC

Thankfully society has made great strides in the area of gender equality. Gone are the days where women were considered property and were thought incapable of doing anything other than housework. Yet the equality of the sexes has made the polite way of interacting with women confusing to some men. Too many fellows mistake equality with absolute sameness and treat a lady like they would any other dude.

Women still want to be treated with class. So set yourself apart from the multitudes of cads out there by practicing the simple but effective art of chivalry.

One caveat: Be attentive to the desires of women. While many women appreciate these gestures, some feel uncomfortable with them. Respect the request of a woman who does not wish to be treated chivalrously.

Open the door. A gentleman will always open and hold the door for a lady. This rule applies to car doors as well, of course. Open the car door, wait until she is seated, then close it. **(FIGURE 4.1)**

Carry a handkerchief. A clean hanky should be a part of every man's arsenal, ready to be handed to a woman in distress. They'll be especially useful at funerals or sad movies.

Retrieve dropped items. The polite thing to do is help pick up a lady's dropped items. Lend your fellow gents a hand, too.

Walk beside a lady on the stairs. Never walk behind a woman on the stairway.

Walk on the outside of a sidewalk. This allows your lady to be farther from the traffic. This way, if someone is going to be splashed, it will be you, not her.

FIGURE 4.1 A gentleman will always open and hold the door for a lady.

Give up your seat. If a lady arrives at a table or boards a subway or bus, and there are no available seats, you should stand up and offer yours to her. This rule also applies to the elderly and physically handicapped of either gender.

Get out of your car. When you pick up a date, get out of the car and come to her door. A honk or call from your cell phone letting her know you have arrived demonstrates a true lack of class.

Introduce her to people. Whenever you run into acquaintances, introduce your date to them. This invites her into the conversation and doesn't leave her standing there in social limbo.

Put on her coat. Always help a lady put on her coat or overgarment. This simple gesture truly marks you as a gentleman.

Make sure she gets home safely. You should always offer to walk or drive her home. If she doesn't feel comfortable having you accompany her, put her in a cab and pay the driver.

Walk her to the door. When the date is over, get out of the car and offer to walk her to the door. Don't presume she wants you to go to the door because she might not yet be comfortable with you doing so. Even if your date declines, still get out of the vehicle, open her car door and bid her good night.

Pay attention to the weather. If the weather is cold and your date is chilly, offer your jacket. If it's raining, hold the umbrella. If it's icy, snowing or pouring rain, play valet and go get the car so she doesn't have to brave the elements.

"A single man has not nearly the value he would have in a state of union. He is an incomplete animal. He resembles the odd half of a pair of scissors."

—BENJAMIN FRANKLIN

Over the past few years, many social observers have noted that young adults are dating less. Instead, dating is being replaced by "hanging out" with members of the opposite sex. Dating and hanging out are two completely different things.

Hanging out consists of people getting together in groups and doing stuff together. The atmosphere is relaxed and relations in the group rarely rise above the level of friendship (or friendship with benefits).

Dating consists of pairing off with someone in a temporary commitment so you can get to know the person better and perhaps start a long-term relationship with them.

There is nothing wrong with hanging out, but it's not a replacement for dating. Dating is the pathway to finding your true love. Love is a one-on-one relationship, so you need to start getting to know women on a one-on-one basis. Bottom line: Start dating and stop hanging out. It really is not that hard to get a date with a woman. Here are some guidelines to remember as you take hanging out up a level to dating.

She wants you to ask. Despite the rhetoric you hear about the liberated woman, women still appreciate when guys ask them on a date. They like when men take the initiative. I've heard lots of successful young professional women lament the fact that men don't ask them out. They're beautiful, smart and charming, but don't have a man. Be a man and ask these women on a date.

Asking is easy. Asking a woman out on a date isn't rocket science. When you ask, though, do it in person or over the phone. If you're poking a woman you're interested in on Facebook, you're a WHITE-LIVERED WEAKLING and lose any credibility as a man.

Keep dates simple. Dates don't have to be elaborate expensive affairs. Keep it simple. If you want to keep things informal, ask her out for lunch or coffee. If you want a more romantic date, have a picnic in the park. The whole point of dating is to get some one-on-one interaction with a woman to find out if she is someone you'd like to start a long-term relationship with. Simple and frequent dates will assist you in this.

Prepare for rejection. Face it. Not every woman you ask out is going to say yes. Prepare for that. It's no big deal if she says no. Think about it. You're no worse off getting rejected than you were before you asked. You didn't have a date with her before, you don't have a date with her now. Your situation has not changed.

MANLY ADVICE

THE BRAD PITT RULE

So you've decided to stop hanging out with women and start dating them. Congrats. But negotiating the waters of dating can be tricky. A little bit of rejection is part of the game, but no man wants to make a frequent habit of it. Fortunately, there's an almost fail proof way to know whether a lady is into you or not. The Brad Pitt Rule. Here's how it works:

Call up the woman you like and ask her on a date. Did she say yes? Great, she probably likes you. What if she makes up an excuse for why she can't go out? Now is the time to employ the Brad Pitt Rule.

Imagine that instead of you, Brad Pitt had asked this same woman out. Would she use the same excuse with him? If Brad Pitt asked her on a date, would she still say she had to study or was going to the movies with friends that night? Nope. She would have dropped pretty much anything and everything to be able to accept a date with Brad.

Now you're not Pitt obviously. But if a woman is interested in you, she will drop her other plans to be available to go out with you.

Of course there are exceptions; the woman may have a legitimate reason she cannot make the date. Perhaps she has to work or go to a funeral. But if this is the case—and here is the real clincher—she will then suggest a different time for the date. She will say something along the lines of, "I can't do it Saturday night; do you want to hang out next weekend instead?"

If she makes up an excuse and she does not suggest an alternative plan, you have been shut out. She is not interested. Do not ask her out again. Doing so will only result in awkwardness and you feeling like an EMASCULATED MASS OF INANITY.

But don't worry, she probably isn't as cool as you thought she was since she doesn't appreciate your charms. Start pursuing another lady who will.

◄ NICE GUYS DON'T HAVE TO FINISH LAST ►

Oftentimes when a man sees yet another bombshell on the arm of a dude who from all appearances is FRAGRANT MAN SWINE, he is compelled to shake his fist at the sky and wonder if there is any justice in the world. "What does she see in him?" he asks in exasperation.

This man believes his well-mannered ways are at the root of the problem, somehow repelling women who inexplicably prefer to date jerks.

But the problem is not that this man is a nice guy; it's that he's allowed his niceness to travel down the slippery slope into weinerdom.

Too many men use their niceness as a cover for the fact that they're insecure. It's this lack of confidence and swagger that kills their chances with the ladies, not their amiable personality. Men often set up a false dichotomy. You can either be an arrogant scallywag or a demure nice guy. But there is a middle ground, the combination women are truly looking for: the extremely confident gentlemen.

BIOLOGY 101

Throughout time and across species, reproductive differences between men and women have led women to be quite choosy when it comes to picking a mate. A male must stand out from the pack to win a female's attention. Whether manifested in an elk's handsome antlers or a caveman's demonstration of hunting prowess, the male must show the female he's a HUCKLEBERRY ABOVE A PERSIMMON.

Happily, the modern man need not strap on some peacock plumage to attract the ladies. Cultivating talent, confidence and mad skills will do the trick just as well.

BECOME THE SUPREMELY CONFIDENT GENTLEMAN

Be a leader and a decision-maker—not a pushover. Yes, couples are equal partners in our modern society. Yes, men should absolutely respect a woman's viewpoint and a couple should strive to make decisions together. But no matter how liberated she is, no woman wants to wear the pants all the time. She doesn't want to be the one who takes care of every single thing. She wants you to take charge sometimes. The reason women sometimes go for total jerks is that they're usually take-charge kinds of guys.

Be ambitious. Primitive women wanted to land the tribe's alpha male, as these men were more likely to be the best providers for their young.

You may no longer need to prove to your lady that you can spear a woolly mammoth, but you still need to show her that you're an alpha male, or at least you're working towards that goal. If you're a corporate guy, show her that you're working your way up to the corner office. If you're a fireman, let her know that you dream of one day becoming the chief.

Have a cool man skill or hobby. Men often have a single-minded fixation on a hobby or interest, and these man passions are really attractive and intriguing to women. I'm not talking about being passionate about collecting *Star Wars* action figures. I'm talking about being really into music and being able to turn your girlfriend on to new bands and burn her CDs you think she'll love. I'm talking about things like woodworking, cooking and guitar playing (on a real guitar, not on *Guitar Hero*). **(FIGURE 4.2)**

FIGURE 4.2 Men often have a single-minded fixation on a hobby or interest, and these man passions are really attractive and intriguing to women.

Not only do cool man skills make you seem interesting and unique, women also like bragging to their friends about you. Remember, women want to feel like they've found a good catch, a man respected by men and envied by women. Napoleon Dynamite was right: Girls like guys with skills.

Be supremely confident about your relationship. A woman wants to feel like you could have had your pick of any woman in the room and you chose her, so never act awestruck by the fact that she actually went out with you or dumbfounded when she says yes to things like a second date or a kiss. Don't constantly express your worry that you might lose her.

Always act like you knew she would say yes and you knew she would fall in love with you from the beginning. There was never a doubt in your mind. Because you're the man, and why wouldn't she fall for you? It's not about being arrogant; it's about being completely confident in what you have to offer a woman.

Be supremely confident and comfortable in your own skin. If you're a little homely, never let on that you think so. If you're a little quirky, act like those quirks make you the coolest man in the room. Witness the curious case of the strange and unattractive starving artist. He doesn't have the looks, the brawn or the money. But women flock to him because a) he's got a cool man skill, b) he's mysterious and c) he's completely comfortable in his skin and couldn't give a rat's behind what people think about him. Radiate the fact that you are wholly and completely your own man.

GIVE FLOWERS LIKE A VICTORIAN GENTLEMAN

Giving a woman flowers is a standard romantic gesture that can help you woo women. But it has unfortunately become a pretty ho-hum cliché. Instead of giving your lady flowers like every other schmo out there, try resurrecting the Victorian tradition of giving flowers. It will infuse the gesture with new life and romance and bring back some of the subtlety, mystery and fun of courtship. **(FIGURE 4.3)**

During the Victorian era, a whole romantic language developed around the giving and receiving of flowers. Everything from the type and size of the flower to the way it was held or presented conveyed layers of meaning and communicated a gentleman's feelings and intentions. Each bouquet contained a secret message for a lady to eagerly interpret and endlessly dissect.

Your lady will swoon that you put far more thought into your selection of flowers than grabbing a bouquet out of the case at Wal-Mart.

FIGURE 4.3 Instead of giving your lady flowers like every other schmo out there, try resurrecting the Victorian tradition of giving flowers.

You'll come off as a real gentleman and a hopeless romantic. Of course, the language of flowers now lies next to Latin in the graveyard of dead discourse. Even in Victorian times, flower meanings were never set in stone and varied from dictionary to dictionary. Therefore, for this tradition to work, you and your love must be using the same source. (You don't want to send a bouquet meant to declare your love and have her interpret it as a message of rejection!) So use the flower list below as your dictionary, and give the cut-out card included in the back to your lady.

MANLY ADVICE

FLOWER MEANINGS

Here's a partial list of meanings to help you get started. Follow them, and you'll need smelling salts to revive your date when she swoons for you.

Ambrosia—Your love is reciprocated
Baby's Breath—Our love is innocent
Camellia, pink—I long for you
Camellia, red—You're a flame in my heart
Camellia, white—You're adorable
Carnation, pink—I will never forget you
Carnation, red—My heart aches for you
Carnation, white—My love is pure
Chrysanthemum, red—I love you
Daffodil—Your feelings are unrequited
Daisy—Love conquers all
Forget-me-not—Remember me forever

Forsythia—I can't wait to see you again

Geranium—I messed up

Gloxinia—It was love at first sight

Hyacinth, purple—I am sorry, please forgive me

Lilac, mauve—Do you still love me?

Lilac, white—You are my first love

Lily, calla—You are beautiful

Primrose—I can't live without you

Rose, orange—I think about you all the time

Rose, pink—Please believe me

Rose, red—I am in passionately in love with you

Rose, red and white together—We're united in our love for each other

Rose, white—You're heavenly

Rose, yellow—Can we be friends?

Sweet Pea—I have to go; good-bye

Tulip, red—I've fallen in love with you

Tulip, yellow—There's sunshine in your smile

Violet, blue—I will always be faithful

Violet, white—Let's take a chance

WHEN TO GIVE FLOWERS

Once you are versed in the language of flowers, you'll be able to create bouquets that will add meaning and significance to any occasion. Here are some times when you'll want to warm your true love's heart with flowers:

Her Birthday. It's her day. Make it extra special by buying her a bouquet of flowers. It doesn't have to be too elaborate.

Your Anniversary. You can't go wrong with buying your wife a bouquet of the same type of flowers you had at your wedding. The very sight of them will create a wave of warm and fuzzy memories. And the fact that you remembered the right flower will send her heart aflutter and score you major romance points.

Valentine's Day. Many women will tell you they don't want anything for Valentine's Day. But this is actually a secret code which means they don't want anything above and beyond flowers. Flowers are so standard as to not even merit mentioning.

New Baby/Mother's Day. Your wife just went through nine months of pain and discomfort to bring forth your progeny. The least you can do is buy her some flowers. Flowers represent new life, and you'll be cradling new life in your arms. Later on, show your wife your appreciation for all the work she puts into mothering by buying flowers each Mother's Day.

Saying I'm Sorry. If you want to get out of the doghouse, bring flowers along with an apology. The extra effort may show the lady in your life that you're really sorry. But make that apology sincere. A bunch of flowers with only a weak or nonexistent apology will backfire; your woman doesn't want to be bought off with cheap gestures. Note: Don't bother with flowers if you've been caught cheating. There aren't enough flowers in the world to cover the stench of a philandering lout.

A Special Date. Whether you are still dating or have been married for years, making time for special dates is essential to keeping your love burning brightly. When planning those romantic outings, put buying flowers on your list of preparations. There's no better way to set the mood for a special night out then to show up at the door with a beautiful bouquet. She'll melt.

Surprise Her. Who says you need a reason to buy the woman in your life flowers? Surprise her! Make it habit to stop by the florist on the way home every now and then to pick up some flowers for your lady.

◄ BREAK UP WITH A WOMAN LIKE A GENTLEMAN ►

Like every variety of trouble, it's easier to get into a relationship than it is to get out of one. Before you find your true love, you'll likely pursue a few relationships that don't work out. Perhaps you discover that she has different values and goals than you. Perhaps your personalities clash too much. You know that the best thing for both of you is to end the relationship. But how do you do it without being a jerk? Even if you don't think this gal is the one for you, she still deserves to be treated with respect. Here are some suggestions on how to break up with a woman like a gentleman.

Make the decision. Before you make a date to tell your gal you're calling it quits, make sure you know for certain that you want to break up. Once you say you want to break up, there's no going back. Also, make sure you know exactly why you're breaking up with her. She deserves to know the reasons for the split.

Tell her in person and let her be the first to know. A gentleman will tell a woman that he wants to break up in person. Don't do it by e-mail, don't text it and especially don't break up with her via Facebook. Only a THOROUGH-PACED SCOUNDREL would do such a thing. She deserves to hear it from you face-to-face. Will it be tough? You bet. But you're a man and men don't shirk from challenges. Also, don't tell your friends/family that you're breaking up with your girlfriend before you tell your girlfriend. Rumors fly. The last thing you want is a confused, angry girlfriend calling you to ask why you're breaking up with her.

Pick a neutral location. Don't break up in familiar settings, like your place, her place or your "favorite" place. You need to find a place where

FIGURE 4.4 There's a good chance your now ex-girlfriend will start crying after you tell her the news. Don't get nervous. Be a rock, but be a sympathetic rock.

the both of you can speak freely. Most men choose restaurants, but that's not always a good idea. At a restaurant you can either tell her at the beginning or at the end of the meal. Either option leaves you with undesirable outcomes. If you do it at the beginning, you might end up awkwardly sitting across from an understandably irate woman while you eat your steak. If you wait until the end, you might back out of your decision. Go to a park or coffee shop instead.

Pick a neutral time. Have the respect of not breaking up with a woman around emotionally significant dates. Her birthday, holidays, your anniversary and especially Valentine's Day are lousy times to break up with a woman. To many women, breaking up on such dates can be seen as a kicking her when she's already down.

Be honest and keep it simple. Don't come up with some long-winded explanation about why you're breaking up with her. It only makes you sound like more of a jerk. Simply tell her the truth of why you're breaking up with her as tactfully and respectfully as you can. Since you already know why you're breaking up, this shouldn't be hard. A woman deserves to know a specific reason for the split; otherwise, she'll be obsessing over the meaning of your cowardly vaguities for a long time to come. Also, let her know this decision was difficult for you. It will slightly cushion the blow; no woman wants to feel like she was easily discarded.

Stay calm. There's a good chance your now ex-girlfriend will start crying after you tell her the news. Don't get nervous. Be a rock, but be a sympathetic rock. No need to get angry or tell her to not make a scene. You'll only make things worse. **(FIGURE 4.4)**

Move on. Once you tell her, move on. Don't say things that may leave open the opportunity to continue the relationship unless you really mean it. For example, don't say "I hope we can be still friends." First, it might give a woman a false sense of hope that there's some way to continue the relationship. Second, most people know this phrase is a bunch of crap. You might as well have said, "It's not you; it's me."

◄ HOW DO YOU KNOW WHEN SHE'S THE ONE? ►

"There is nothing nobler or more admirable than when two people who see eye to eye keep house as man and wife, confounding their enemies and delighting their friends."

—HOMER

So how do you know if you're picking the right woman to settle down with? Some men agonize over the decision, afraid the wrong choice will leave them trapped in a loveless marriage or scarred by a bitter divorce. The truth is that knowing you've found the right woman to marry is not rocket science. It can honestly be one the easiest decisions of your life. Here are four guidelines that will let you know if your woman is the one.

The relationship goes smoothly from the beginning. The best relationships happen completely naturally from start to finish. The couple meets, they get along swimmingly, they start dating and then they get married. The courtship process is not saddled with DTRs (Define the Relationship talks), frequent fighting and numerous breakups and reconciliations. This is not to say that men in such volatile relationships shouldn't get hitched. But the volatility will most likely continue into the marriage. Whether that volatility is acceptable is up to each individual man and his sense of the strength of that relationship.

She gets along well with your family and friends. There are exceptions to this rule: Your girlfriend and one of your friends or family members may simply have clashing personality traits. But in general, it's a red flag if your girlfriend does not mix well with your loved ones. Think

FIGURE 4.5 If you feel like your girlfriend is your best friend in the world, there is a very good chance that she is the one for you.

about it–your family raised you and made you who you are, and you picked your friends based on your common interests and values. If she doesn't like them and they don't like her, then it may mean you're not seeing something important about your girlfriend that they do. Love often blurs your vision and judgment. Your loved ones have an outsider's perspective on the relationship. This doesn't mean you should break up with a woman just because your friends and family don't like her. If you're sure of your relationship, be confident in moving forward with it. But it's wise to seek honest feedback from others.

There is nothing major you want to change about her. There will always be differences and conflicts in a relationship. But if there is something truly significant about your girlfriend that you wish she would change, that is a red flag. In the initial stages of a relationship, when your brain is bathed with love chemicals, you may be willing to overlook the flaw or even find it strangely endearing. But after several years, when the love chemicals have ebbed, this trait may begin to grate on your soul. Remember, people seldom change, and marriage won't magically resolve your issues.

She's your best friend. Physical attraction and chemistry are obviously crucial to any relationship. But at the core of the relationship should be a strong and deeply rooted friendship. Forty years down the line you're both going to be soft, wrinkly and saddled with low libidos. The thing that will hold your marriage together when you're old and gray is your friendship. Therefore, if you feel like your girlfriend is your best friend in the world, there is a very good chance that she is the one for you. Do you want to spend all your time with her? Does she make any situation from going to a ballgame to doing your taxes more enjoyable? Do you feel like you could tell her anything and that she knows more about you than anyone in the world? Yes? Well then, she's a keeper. **(FIGURE 4.5)**

Lately marriage has gotten a bad rap. It seems like many men these days feel marriage is an archaic arrangement that holds them back from realizing their full potential. Even if men aren't particularly anti-marriage, they will avoid getting hitched for as long as they can.

Men often delay marriage because they believe that dating and cohabitation offer all of the benefits (particularly sex) of marriage without the commitment and responsibility. They are fooling themselves. Nearly all of the true advantages of marriage (yes, even sex) apply only to actual married couples, not those couples living together, and certainly not to those simply dating.

While it is seriously unwise for men to rush into marriage willy-nilly, once you've found your true love and you're sure she's the one, there's no reason to delay your nuptials. Why? Marriage offers truly significant benefits that cannot be found outside of it. Here are six reasons you should grow up, man up and stopping being so scared of walking down the aisle.

THE BENEFITS OF MARRIAGE

"Marriage is our last, best chance to grow up."

—JOSEPH BARTH

More and better sex. The popular belief is that marriage stifles sexual fulfillment. The reality is that married men are having better and more frequent sex than their single buddies who go to clubs each weekend trolling for a woman who's willing to take them home. Married sex is even better than cohabitation sex; 50 percent of married men find their sex life physically and emotionally fulfilling, compared to only 38 percent of cohabiting couples. Married sex produces an environment of trust and openness, allowing couples to honestly express their sexual needs and desires to their spouse. This results in better, more satisfying whoopee.

More money. Married men are wealthier men. Married men earn between 10 and 40 percent more than single men. They also receive promotions more frequently and earn more glowing performance reviews than their single coworkers. Employers often see married men as more settled and responsible than their single counterparts.

Better health. Married men are healthier men. They stay healthier and live longer than their single or cohabiting peers. Just how much healthier are they? Take a look at these statistics:

- Married men have fewer infections and a lower risk of heart disease and some cancers.
- Married men are less likely to smoke, drink heavily and be physically inactive.
- Married men are less likely to suffer from health conditions like back pain, headaches and serious psychological distress.
- Single people spend longer in the hospital and have a greater risk of dying after surgery.
- Nine out of 10 married men who are alive at age 48 are alive at age 65. Only 6 out of 10 single men who were alive at age 48 are alive at 65.
- On average, married men live 10 years longer than single men. A whole decade!

A bigger smile. Married men are happier than their single counterparts. One study showed that 40 percent of married people said they were generally happy with their life, while only 25 percent of single people said they were. The bigger smile might be due in part to married men getting more sex than their single peers. But marriage also provides incomparable companionship and forces people to commit to something bigger than themselves, which contributes to happiness.

True companionship. There is an old Swedish proverb that says, "Shared joy is double joy. Shared sorrow is half sorrow." Truer words have seldom been spoken. Marriage basically means always having your best friend around. Everything from going to the gym to grocery shopping is ten times more enjoyable when your wife is by your side.

Your wife is there in the middle of the night when your worries are keeping you up; she's there when you get off work and need to unload the frustrations of your day; she's there to give you a pep talk over the breakfast table on the day you have a big presentation. No matter how loyal a friend is, they're not family. They move, they ditch you when they have a hot date, they distance themselves when you have a big fight. You and your wife made a vow to be together forever; it's wonderful to absolutely know that someone has your back come hell or high water.

Finally, remember that marriage can be as happy as you want it to be.

With the divorce rate hovering around 50 percent, many men view marriage as too risky a chance to take. But marriage is not a lottery, nor is it a game of Russian roulette. You don't get married and then cross your fingers that you don't become one of the statistics. Divorce is not a disease that some people catch and some people have immunity to. There is no more erroneous idea than that of "falling out of love." Nobody falls out of love. One or both partners stop working at their relationship, and they give up. Be absolutely sure you pick the right woman to marry, someone who will be just as passionately committed to making the marriage work as you are, and your chances of having a happy marriage are nearly 100 percent.

◀ ASKING FOR A WOMAN'S HAND IN MARRIAGE ▶

Once you know your gal is the one for you and you're ready to take the plunge with her, there is an important duty you must take care of before you propose: asking your future father-in-law for his daughter's hand in marriage. It is a tradition that has unfortunately been slowly fading away from Western society. Many argue that the whole idea smacks of sexism and chauvinism and harks back to times when women were treated like chattel.

Quite not. You're not making a property exchange, you're asking for her father's blessing. When you get hitched, you're not only marrying your honey, you're also marrying into her family. Asking for her family's blessing gets your relationship with them off on the right foot. It's a profoundly respectful gesture that lets the family know you're sincere in your intentions and a true gentleman.

But it's definitely not an easy task; the experience can make any man a nervous wreck. Following these guidelines will help ease the stress and make this rite of passage bearable if not enjoyable.

1. Talk to your girlfriend first. Before you do anything, make sure you and your girlfriend are on the same page about a few things. First, is she ready to commit? Does she even want to get married? You don't want to get her father's blessing only to have her GIVE YOU THE MITTEN. Second, ask your girlfriend how she feels about you seeking her dad's blessing. While traditionally this is a man-to-man talk between prospective husband and future father-in-law, a modern woman may desire that you speak with both of her parents. Or your girlfriend's dad may have passed away or been an absent or abusive father, and she may ask that you speak only to her mother. If so, be sure to honor her wishes.

2. Try to meet her father before you ask. If it's possible, try to meet your girlfriend's parents a few times before you decide to ask for the blessing. Having established a relationship will make sitting down with Dad and discussing your wish to marry his daughter a bit easier. Again, not all situations will allow this, but if you can, do it.

3. Sit down with him man-to-man. There are several ways you can go about this, and I think it all depends on what kind of man your girlfriend's father is. Consider taking him out to dinner or going to a bar or coffee shop. Breaking bread with him might make the situation a bit more comfortable. If that's not a possibility, during a visit simply ask if you can speak to him in private. If her dad lives far away, try to time the conversation for a trip home which has already been planned, perhaps during the holidays. If this is not possible, it's okay to conduct the talk over the phone.

4. Start out expressing your feelings for his daughter. Begin the conversation by expressing to your girlfriend's father the love and admiration you have for his daughter. Tell him how much she means to you. Mention some specific qualities that you love about her. He raised her, so you are really complimenting him at the same time.

5. Explain your wish to marry his daughter. Now it's time to cut to the chase. Assure him that you understand the seriousness of the commitment and that being able to spend the rest of your life with his daughter would make you the happiest man in the world.

6. Promise him you'll take care of his daughter for the rest of her life. Put yourself in this man's shoes. He's been the man in her life since she was a baby. He's taken care of her since she was in diapers and only wants the best for her. He wants to know that he's handing off his little girl to someone who will take just as good care of her as he has. Make the commitment that you'll always provide for, honor, respect and cherish his daughter.

7. Respectfully ask for his blessing. It's time to request his blessing and support in proposing to his daughter.

"It is not a lack of love, but a lack of friendship that makes unhappy marriages."
—FRIEDRICH NIETZSCHE

All your dating, wooing and chivalry won't mean a thing if you cheat on your wife and let the life and love you created together slip away. Twenty-five percent of all American men (and some studies put the number far higher) will have extramarital affairs during their lifetime. Will you be one of the four? Or will you stay true?

Many people look at infidelity as if it was a natural disaster. No one could see it coming. It just inexplicably happened. The truth is that not only can men see it coming, they can prevent it from happening as well.

It is possible to affair-proof your marriage. Will it be a lot of work? Yes. But that's what you signed up for when you decided to marry your sweetheart.

Keep dating your wife. Establish a weekly "date night" with your wife and treat this time as sacred. Your dates don't have to be fancy, but you do need to work to keep them fresh. A recent study showed that injecting novelty into your dates can bring back the butterflies you experienced when you were first courting. So visit a new restaurant, try a new hobby or take a class together.

Focus on being romantic. Any woman will tell you it doesn't take much to be romantic. A romantic letter or e-mail only takes a few minutes to write. Flowers are easy to buy. These small gestures show your wife that you're thinking about her during the day and help reinforce your commitment.

Initiate affection. Studies show that couples who are affectionate with each other stay together. Make an effort to initiate spontaneous affection with your wife. Give her a hug or surprise kiss and tell her how much you love her. Hold hands when you're out together. Invite cuddling with her without making it a precursor to sex. These small gestures will help strengthen the physical connection that every relationship needs.

Have sex regularly. Many men stray because they've gotten bored with their sex life with their wife. It's pretty easy to get into a bedroom slump when you're married. Things get busy and by the end of the day couples are just too tired for it. Make sex with your wife a priority. It doesn't have to involve kama sutra and edible underwear. Just do it. Frequent sexual encounters with your wife will strengthen your emotional and physical attraction to her.

Spend time just talking. Find some time each day to have meaningful conversations with your wife. If you have kiddos, do it after you put them in bed. Talk about what you did during the day, what you've been thinking about lately and your hopes for the future. These conversations will deepen the bond between to you and your wife.

Share a common interest. A big reason men stray from their wives is that they begin to find less and less in common with them. Once jobs and kids intervene with your once simple coupledom, there may begin to be fewer areas of your lives which overlap.

Avoid this by maintaining a common interest or hobby with your wife. Take dance lessons, train for a marathon or read the same books. Just find something that both of you can enjoy and participate in together.

Have a sense of honor and duty. Remember that when you got married you made a sacred promise or vow that you would be faithful to your wife. There was a time when a gentleman was judged on whether or not he was a man of his word. Sadly people today don't take those sorts of things seriously. Many people feel justified in breaking their promises when something stops being easy and pleasurable. Buck the trend. Be a man of honor and integrity.

CHAPTER FIVE

◀|▶ THE ◀|▶
FATHER

"Fatherhood is pretending the present
you love most is soap-on-a-rope."
—BILL COSBY

Being a dad is perhaps the manliest job you'll ever have. It's a role that requires you to call upon hundreds of manly skills and attributes. You have to display leadership, manly compassion and strength. You have to know how to fish, build forts and even how to braid little girls' hair. (Braiding is like knot tying. It's manly.)

The world is in need of good fathers. Studies have shown that children who have involved fathers do better in school, are more self-confident and have better social connections with their peers. Boys that have good relationships with their fathers show fewer behavioral problems than boys that don't. Sadly, for the past 40 years, men have been neglecting their fatherly duties. Many men abandon their families and leave a woman to raise their children on their own. Even men who don't abandon their families physically, do so emotionally. They'd rather spend time at the office or at their buddy's house playing poker than spend time with their kids and get involved with their lives. This is one of the reasons we wanted to write this book: In too many cases, fathers have stopped passing down the art of manliness to the next generation.

Dad-manship does not come with an instruction manual. And of course you can't put everything that a man needs to know about being a dad in a book. Learning to be a dad is mainly a function of trial and error. However, we've included some advice on getting started and a few of the most pertinent things all dads and future dads should know. Make it your goal to have your children say about you what Theodore Roosevelt said about his father: "My father was the best man I ever knew. He combined strength and courage with gentleness, tenderness, and great unselfishness. He would not tolerate in us children selfishness or cruelty, idleness, cowardice, or untruthfulness." As a father, you are the crucial link in passing down the art of manliness to your children.

Despite the great strides made in the area of gender equality, there's one thing that women can do that you'll never be able to: grow a baby. You're never going to know how it feels to be pregnant or give birth to your precious progeny. But that doesn't mean you shouldn't have an active part in the gestation process. You and your wife are a team, and there's many things you can do to be a supremely supportive dad-to-be.

Respond appropriately to the news she's pregnant. If you weren't planning on a bundle of joy entering your life, make sure you don't respond in a way that shows you're not excited about the news. Inappropriate responses would include: breaking down and crying tears of agony, making a face of disgust or asking why she wasn't using her birth control. You want your wife to feel confident and secure that you'll be

FIGURE 5.1 Read some books on pregnancy. The more you know about what she's going through, the better equipped you are to empathize and know how to help.

there for her during these trying nine months and that you're willing to step up and be a great dad.

Read some books on pregnancy. Knowledge is power. The more you know about what she's going through, the better equipped you are to empathize and know how to help. There are hundreds of pregnancy books to choose from. *What to Expect When You're Expecting* is a classic and guides you through what your wife is experiencing during each step of her pregnancy. **(FIGURE 5.1)**

Accompany her to doctor's appointments. This serves three purposes. First and most importantly, it shows your wife that you're with her all the way in the pregnancy. Second, you'll know exactly what's going on with her pregnancy and will be better prepared to help her. Finally, seeing your baby's picture, even when it looks like an indistinguishable lump, and hearing its heartbeat will help create a fetus/father bond. Even if you're terribly busy at work or school, always make time for a doctor's appointment.

Help her through morning sickness. Morning sickness is quite possibly the worst part of pregnancy (well, besides that whole labor thing). It strikes about 75 percent of all pregnant women. Symptoms of morning sickness include headaches, excessive sleepiness and of course feelings of nausea and sometimes vomiting. Most women will start feeling the symptoms of morning sickness about a month after conception, and it will typically last until the twelfth to fourteenth week of pregnancy. Some women will experience morning sickness their entire pregnancy. Despite its name, morning sickness doesn't happen only in the morning. Most women experience the symptoms of morning sickness all day long. When helping her through this rocky period, the key is to keep experimenting with different remedies. Introduce new treatments each day to see which work for her and which don't. Be willing to make many trips, sometimes late at night, in search of something else to ease her troubles. Here are a few remedies that might do the trick:

- Vitamin B6 supplements. Studies have shown that vitamin B6 supplements can alleviate the symptoms of morning sickness.

- Seasickness bracelets. Seasickness bracelets are elastic bands with plastic bumps that apply pressure to points on the wrist. Supposedly this pressure can reduce the feelings of nausea.

- Ginger ale. The fizziness of ginger ale or any other clear soda can help with nausea. And ginger has been shown to reduce the symptoms of morning sickness. So ginger ale is a winning combo. Most popular brands of ginger ale don't have any real ginger in them; look for smaller, independent brands that still use the real McCoy.

- Crackers. The problem with morning sickness is that your wife will not feel like eating much, but an empty stomach will only make the feelings of nausea worse. Crackers are easy on the stomach and can stave off the nausea that starts in the morning. Have her eat some before she even gets out of bed.

- Ginger or peppermint tea. As with ginger, peppermint has been shown to help reduce the feelings of nausea associated with morning sickness.

- Be flexible. Some foods will be totally unappetizing to your wife one day, and the next it will be the only thing that appeals to her. Be flexible and give her whatever her stomach will keep down. Be willing to run out and buy whatever she craves.

- Keep yourself clean. Pregnant women become hypersensitive to smells. Even scents she once enjoyed can now start her stomach churning. So brush your teeth and shower daily, or she may not be able to stand having you around.

Reduce her stress. Pregnancy is physically and emotionally demanding, so don't burden your wife with any unneeded pressure. Take on more of the household chores like cleaning, cooking and grocery shopping so your wife can rest. However, when you take on these responsibilities make sure to do them right. Ruining your wife's favorite shirt in the wash will negate any stress reduction your good deed might have garnered.

Be patient. Pregnancy totally wreaks havoc on your wife's hormones. Some days she'll feel fantastic, some days she'll bite your head off as soon as you open your mouth and some days she'll break down and cry for no reason at all. Be patient and recognize that it's the hormones. Also, be understanding when it comes to your love life. Your wife's sex drive will be all over the place during her pregnancy: often plummeting in the first trimester, bouncing back in the second and falling again in the third. Patience, friend, patience.

Tell her she's beautiful and that you love her. Your wife will be undergoing some serious body transformations during pregnancy. Reassure her that you think she's beautiful and that you love her immensely. Affirm your unwavering dedication to her each and every day.

DELIVER A BABY IN A PINCH

The arrival of your little one may not wait for the man in the white coat or weather conditions may prevent you from driving the Mrs. to the hospital. As a man, you should be prepared for such situations by knowing how to deliver a baby. Here's how to do it.

1. Don't panic. Your wife is under a lot of stress right now. Standing there HAVY CAVY or running around the house yelling like a little boy will not help her. Ease her stress by remaining completely calm.

2. Assess the situation. During labor your wife will experience con-tractions—the periodic tightening and relaxing of her uterine muscle. You'll know your wife is experiencing one by the looks of discomfort on her face. If your wife's contractions are less than two minutes apart, the baby is on its way, and you probably don't have time to get to the doctor. If you can see the top of the baby's head in the vagina, you definitely don't have time.

3. Call for help. Just because you read something in a book or watched Coco give birth to puppies when you were eight, does not make you an expert on delivering babies. Call an ambulance. Even if the baby comes before it gets there, someone can talk you through the process. **(FIGURE 5.2)**

4. Get Mom comfortable. Because you've seen hundreds of television and movie births, your first reaction will probably be to have Mom lie on

FIGURE 5.2 Call an ambulance. Even if the baby comes before it gets there, someone can talk you through the process.

her back. This position isn't actually the most comfortable or effective for delivery. If space is available, have her get on her hands and knees. This alleviates some of the pressure on her back. Some women also find it comfortable to stand or squat when giving birth, positions which allow gravity to aid in the birthing process. Just let nature dictate what she does. If Mom is in one of these vertical positions, keep an eye on the baby so he or she doesn't squirm out into a free fall. If space isn't available (say, in the back of a taxicab), the traditional on-the-back position will suffice.

5. Scrub up and prepare the birthing area. You don't want to risk giving the baby or Mom an infection by handling them with your grubby paws. Wash your hands and arms with hot water and plenty of antibacterial soap. Birth is a messy process, so make sure you place clean sheets or a shower curtain under Mom. You'll also need to have some clean towels handy to wipe off and wrap up the newly arrived bundle of joy. If you're in a taxi, you can use your shirt.

6. Watch and guide. Nature is pretty dang amazing. For the most part the baby doesn't need much assistance to make it into the world. Avoid barking instructions for your wife to push and breathe. You'll just stress her out and cause her to possibly push when she shouldn't. Let her push when it feels natural. When the head makes it out of the vagina, the baby will turn to one side. That's completely normal. He or she is just trying to get in the best position to make an escape. Simply place your hand under the baby's head and gently guide it downward. Don't try to speed the process along by pulling on the baby. Just gently guide the shoulders out, one at a time. As the baby makes his entrance into the world, be ready to receive him; babies are slippery!

7. Rub the baby down. Take that clean towel and gently rub the baby down to clean off the fluid and blood. The rubbing will also help stimulate the baby so it starts breathing. Wipe any fluids out of its nose and mouth. If you have a straw, take it and suction out the fluids by inserting the straw into the nostril and then placing your finger on the open end. No need for holding it upside down and slapping its tush. That practice went away along with polio and celebratory cigars in the waiting room. Just place the baby, skin to skin, on Mom's stomach and cover the new arrival with a towel or shirt.

8. Don't cut or tie the cord. Wait for a trained professional to do this.

9. Deliver the placenta. About fifteen to thirty minutes after the baby is delivered, Mom will expel the placenta, the sack that's been nurturing your baby for the past five months. When you see the placenta start coming out, don't pull on it to make it come out faster; just let it slip out naturally. If it's not coming out right away, you can massage the mother's abdomen to help it along.

10. Get medical attention ASAP. By now the ambulance should be there. If not, get Mom and new baby to the hospital as soon as possible so doctors can take care of the umbilical cord and examine the goods.

11. Bully for you! You're a dad. And you didn't even have to boil any water!

◀ CHANGE A DIAPER ▶

A new baby is a poop and pee machine. You'll be amazed that such a small person can produce so much waste. With a newborn, you can expect to change a diaper every two hours. That's twelve changes in a single twenty-four-hour day! Wowza! As the baby gets older, the changings will get less frequent, but you'll still be plowing through a lot of diapers. Unfortunately science has yet to create a self-cleaning baby, so it's up to you and your wife to clean your little champ/princess and keep their waste-producing faculties in shipshape condition. If you're working while your wife is at home, she'll probably be saddled with much of the diaper-changing responsibility; a dirty diaper waits for no man. But whenever you're home, you need to put that clothespin on your nose and get to work.

1. Assess the damage. If you smell something funky, you know you need to change your little turd machine's diaper. When you go to check the damage, be prepared for anything. You might have just a small little nugget waiting for you, or you could have a runny, hazardous waste explosion that has left the confines of the diaper. If it's the latter, it's best to move the baby near the bath, so you can thoroughly clean him or her.

2. Get your materials. Grab a clean diaper and five or six baby wipes. Place them to the side.

3. Put your gas mask on and assume the position. If your baby is formula fed, be prepared for a gut-wrenching, nauseating smell. If your baby is breastfed, the smell isn't quite as bad. If you have boy, it's always a good idea to juke to the side lest his little sprinkler baptize you into the Church of the Yellow Stream.

4. Undo the dirty diaper and lift your baby's butt off the diaper. Lifting of the tukus can be done by grabbing your baby's ankles and gently lifting their feet into the air. Use a clean part of the dirty diaper to wipe any excess poo from the baby's behind.

5. Wipe. With your baby's little butt lifted off the ground, grab a baby wipe and start wiping front to back. The front to back motion reduces the chance of spreading bacteria into their privates, which can cause a urinary tract infection. Make sure you don't miss a spot. Place the used wipes on top of the soiled diaper. Then, with your baby's feet still suspended in the air, remove the soiled diaper.

6. Close the dirty diaper and dispose. Fold the diaper on itself with the hazardous waste and used wipes still in it. Use the sticky tabs to make a tight bundle. Hook shot the used diaper into the diaper bin.

7. Slide the new diaper under your progeny. In order for a diaper to function correctly, it needs to be on right. If you have it on backwards, you'll have a bigger mess to clean next time. The back of the diaper has the sticky tabs on it. Lay your baby down on this part.

8. Check for rashes and treat accordingly. If your baby has a case of diaper rash, apply some ointment to it.

9. Pat dry. If you want to avoid diaper rashes, make sure your baby's bottom is nice and dry. With a name like "baby powder" you'd think a little of that white stuff would be just the thing, but it isn't. Powder can cause potential lung problems if your baby inhales it. Try cornstarch instead.

10. Bring up the front of the diaper and attach the tabs. You want it tight enough so that it doesn't slide off but not so tight it cuts off circulation to your baby's legs. Most disposable diapers have little ruffles around the leg. Make sure those are sticking out, or you'll have some leaking problems.

11. Give your baby a high five.

◄ QUIET A CRYING BABY ►

"Being a great father is like shaving. No matter how good you shaved today, you have to do it again tomorrow."

—REED MARKHAM

Before you became a new dad, you probably imagined fatherhood idyllically, with you holding an ever-smiling, giggling, cooing baby. When it's 3 A.M. and your baby once again rouses you from sleep with his supersonic cries, the reality of being a dad sets in. You walk to the crib, look down, and wonder, "Short of throwing him out the window, how can I get this little person to be quiet?" With a little practice and some know-how, you'll be able to calm your baby's CATERWAULS so you and your wife can get a bit more sleep at night and a tad more sanity during the day.

WHY IS THIS KID CRYING?!

Although it might seem like it, babies don't generally cry for the heck of it. Babies cry when they need something. It's their only form of communication for a year and a half. So the first step in quieting your baby is to decipher the source of their wailing.

After you get to know your baby, you might be able to sense subtle differences in his cries indicating that he wants certain things. Until you achieve that sort of familiarity, it's basically going to be trial and error in discovering what's irking your scream machine.

Below we've included some common reasons a baby cries and what you can do to remedy the problem.

Hungry. If your baby just woke up or has a full load in his pants, his tummy is probably empty. Give him to Mom or give him a bottle.

Tired. If your baby's crying has lots of intermittent yawning, the little guy is probably tuckered out. Lay him down for a nap.

Discomfort. Just like you, your baby gets too hot or too cold. Unlike you, your baby can't adjust the thermostat or strip down to his diaper. Also, laying in your own urine and fecal matter isn't very comfortable. If it feels too cold or hot, adjust the temp. If your baby has soiled his diaper, change it.

Sickness. When your baby's sick, the cry might be more of a whimper. Check him to see if he has a fever or other signs of illness, and if the symptoms are serious, call your doctor.

Overstimulation. Sometimes things just get too crazy for your baby. The womb was a pretty boring place, so a baby's brain can only take so much stimulation. Whisk the little guy to a quiet place and rock the jitters away.

Loneliness. The world is a big confusing place for your new baby. If he wakes up and no one familiar is around, he'll start to feel lonely. He can't seek solace by listening to The Cure, so in the beginning, pick him up and hang out with him. Then gradually teach him to soothe himself by going in less often and letting him cry himself to sleep.

Fussiness. If you've got a persnickety baby on your hands, stick a pacifier in her mouth, or put on some soothing music. Some parents have had success taking their little one for a drive in the back of a car. Anyone who's been on a road trip knows that the moving automobile has a very womb-like quality to it.

MANLY ADVICE

WHAT IF I HAVE A COLICKY BABY?

If your baby keeps CATERWAULING no matter what you do, you might have a colicky baby on your hands. Colicky babies have predictable, reoccurring and intense crying fits that last for hours. Your baby may also clench his fists and bring his legs into his stomach. To quiet a colicky baby, you need an attack plan. Here's yours:

Swaddle him like baby Jesus. Get a blanket and wrap your baby up in a little baby burrito. This will make him feel warm and secure. Black beans and salsa are optional. **(FIGURE 5.3)**

Rock her. Gently rock your baby. If your arms get tired, strengthen them by doing push-ups. In the meantime, let technology do the work for you by putting your baby in one of those automatic rockers.

Create some white noise. It's counterintuitive, but many babies need noise to fall asleep. The womb was a noisy place with all those bodily fluids flowing hither and thither. While rocking your swaddled baby, make a "shhhhh" noise. If that doesn't work, try running the vacuum cleaner or put your baby near the clothes dryer. You can also take your baby for a late-night drive. Pick up some Taco Bell for yourself while you're out.

Give him the pacifier. Sucking on things can be comforting to a baby. Stick a pacifier into his wailing mouth and let the magical plastic teat quickly soothe his manic cries.

FIGURE 5.3 Get a blanket and wrap your baby up in a little baby burrito. This will make him feel warm and secure.

◄ BALANCE WORK AND FAMILY ►

"For unflagging interest and enjoyment, a household of children, if things go reasonably well, certainly all other forms of success and achievement lose their importance by comparison."

—THEODORE ROOSEVELT

Back in your grandpa's time, a man was just expected to bring home the bacon and was excused from being too hands-on in the child rearing department. Today's man is expected to be both a provider and a highly involved parent. These two demands can burn out even the strongest of men. Here are a few suggestions on how to be a corporate warrior and a superdad at the same time.

Have family dinner. Studies have shown children from families that have meals together do better in school and are less likely to get involved with drugs. Make it home each evening to have dinner with your family. If this means getting to work extra early in the morning, so be it. At mealtime, ask about what's going on in your kid's life. If you can get home early enough, cook dinner with your kids.

Take each kid out once a month for dad time. Each month, set aside a date night for each kid. Take them out individually and do something they enjoy. It's a great way to get one-on-one time with each kid and ensure that jealousy between siblings remains in check.

Limit work on weekends and holidays. Try to devote your time off from work to your family. Sure, you'll have to spend time doing chores and running errands to get ready for the next week, but you can kill two birds (and rake many more leaves) by getting your children involved with those tasks.

Use your vacation. Many Americans are WORKING LIKE GRAVE DIGGERS and taking less and less of their vacation time. Don't be one of these men. Use your full two weeks and take your family on the great American road trip or on a camping adventure in a national park. Don't bring along your laptop or Blackberry. Family vacations will be some of your kids' best childhood memories. Don't deny them these experiences by being a workaholic.

Take your kid to work with you for the day. You'll get to spend some quality bonding time together. And your kid will see what Dad does all day and will better understand why you can't be home all the time.

Make it to all your kids' activities. Even if this means bringing some work with you to do during the time-outs and halftime of their football game, at least you are there. It will mean a lot to your kid to see their dad in the stands rooting them on.

Schedule a weekly Family Night. Make this a nonnegotiable date, and schedule all other activities around it. Play board games, watch a video or go out and get some ice cream.

Tuck your kids in bed and read them a book. Bedtimes routines aren't just for tykes. Even when your kid gets older, make it a tradition to read to them. You can move from *The Very Hungry Caterpillar* to *Treasure Island* as they grow up. **(FIGURE 5.4)**

FIGURE 5.4 Bedtimes routines aren't just for tykes. Even when your kid gets older, make it a tradition to read to them.

"It is easier to build strong children than to repair broken men."

—FREDERICK DOUGLASS

Today it's hard not to notice that kids are becoming less resilient and more clueless on how to survive in the real world. There's a proliferation of UNLICKED CUBS that whine when they don't get what they want and think they are entitled to all the comforts of the world without having to lift a finger. As a dad, you can prevent the wussification of your children. Here are six ways fathers can raise strong, resilient, independent children.

1. Give them some independence. Kids can't venture a half a mile from their homes these days without parents worrying for their safety. This culture of obsessive overprotectiveness is bred by the media. As the twenty-four-hour news networks and people like Nancy Grace regurgitate stories of abduction over and over and over again, it begins to seem like the world outside your suburban castle is a very dangerous place indeed. Yet the reality is very different from how the media spins it. The chance of your child being taken by a stranger is more than one in a million, and 90 percent of sexual abuse cases are committed by someone the victim knows. There's a far greater chance of your child dying in the SUV you pick him up from school in than there is in letting him walk home.

So don't coddle your kids by keeping them under lock and key and only letting them out if you can keep a constant eye on them. You're squelching their development and sense of independence. Teach your kids how to stay out of trouble and away from strangers, and then turn them loose to ride their bikes, roam the neighborhoods, run errands and walk to school by themselves.

2. Let them do unsafe things. Everything today is childproof and fun proof. Have you been to a playground lately? Did you notice what was missing? Teeter-totters, merry-go-rounds and sometimes even swings are going extinct, replaced by plastic-coated, low-to-the-ground snooze-inducing apparatuses. Some playgrounds even have signs that say "no running." I kid you not. While these changes are often pushed by city managers worried about liability, parents are equally at fault in trying to clear any dangers from the path of their children. They fail to understand that while sticking kids in a protective bubble may keep them safe in the short term, it leaves them more vulnerable down the road. Some lessons in safety must be learned from trial and error. If children don't learn to deal with dangerous tools and situations growing up, when they finally leave the nest, they may lack the skills necessary to negotiate the real world.

3. Don't be their best friend. While many parents today strive to be their children's best friend, this is fundamentally the wrong way to raise a child. Parents want to believe they can be their child's bosom buddy because they enjoy such a healthy, close relationship. The reality is that parents want to be their child's buddy because they're afraid of their kid not liking them. But parenting is not a popularity contest. Being a true parent means that sometimes you have to lay down the rules, and oftentimes your kid is not going to like it. While tough love may be painful for both child and parent in the short term, it greatly benefits both in the long term. Kids don't need a pal; they need an authority figure. Deep down, they *do* want someone to give them boundaries and structure. Best friends are equals; parents and children are not. If you insist on being your kids' best friend, a situation will inevitably arise where you finally try to reign them in and make them respect you. But it will be too late; they'll feel free to toss your advice aside like they would for any friend. **(FIGURE 5.5)**

4. Don't automatically take their side. While it's natural to think the best of your children, don't be overly defensive when others criticize them. Teachers and friends typically do not have ulterior motives

FIGURE 5.5 Parenting is not a popularity contest. Being a true parent means that sometimes you have to lay down the rules, and oftentimes your kid is not going to like it.

when sharing a story of your child's misbehavior. As outside observers, they may have valuable insight into something about your kid that you have overlooked and need to address. Your child needs to earn your trust, just as anyone else does. Don't give it to them automatically.

5. Make them work for what they get. If children are not given responsibilities and work at a young age, it's harder to instill the ethic when they're older. You're doing your child a great disservice if you buy every stinking thing they want. Sure, it's easier to buy them the ten dollar toy just to shut down their tantrum. But all you're doing is conditioning them to the idea that if you whine enough, you'll get what you want.

By encouraging your children to work for what they get, you'll be teaching them essential skills they will carry with them the rest of their life. Not only will they develop an appreciation for work, they'll learn valuable lessons in money management, responsibility and initiative.

During the early 1900s, kids were working sixty hours a week in factories and coal mines. While it was a deplorable situation, it shows that kids are capable of taking on far greater tasks than parents today are willing to give them. They may no longer have to break slate, but they can at least clean the bathroom and mow the lawn.

6. Don't praise them indiscriminately. What's the point of an award if everyone gets one? What's the point in striving to be your best, if everyone is equally rewarded? In such situations, praise loses all of its meaning, even for those who really deserve it. Every parent believes their kid is special; that's natural. But if you heap enormous and unwarranted praise on your kids, it's going to end up debilitating them. Praising your child indiscriminately sends the message that praise is not earned, it is something one is naturally entitled to. And it will end up dissolving their competitive drive. These children grow up believing they can do anything and everything well. As adults, they become restless at every job, forever unsure of which field is best suited for their "infinite" talents.

The reality is that there are certain things we are good at, and certain things we are not. If you praise your kids for everything, they'll have a harder time honing in on their true abilities and strengths. So instead of praising them indiscriminately, center your praise on specific achievements. For example, say, "You did a great job on your math test." Not, "You are so smart and wonderful!"

◀ TEACH YOUR KID TO RIDE A BIKE ▶

It's a rite of passage every child must go through—learning how to ride a bike. While the path to bike riding mastery is often strewn with scraped elbows and bruised knees, it's a skill they'll never forget. As their dad, you have the honor of guiding your child through one of suburbia's most important coming-of-age rituals. Here's how you can quickly get your child up, riding and experiencing the most exhilarating sense of freedom a six-year-old can enjoy: pedaling away from their parents.

Start 'em young with a tricycle. Get your kid a tricycle when he's just a few years old. The tricycle will teach him two important biking skills: steering and pedaling. What's great about tricycles is that they can be used inside, so your kid can practice his skills on the safety of your hardwood floors (provided Mom approves).

Graduate to training wheels. Once your child has the steering and pedaling thing down, it's time to upgrade to a bike with training wheels. Training wheels enable her to learn two additional biking skills: balance and braking. Find a bike that's appropriate for her height and attach the training wheels. The key to effectively using training wheels is to gradually adjust their height. When first starting out, angle the wheels so that they are in constant contact with the ground. This provides maximum stability for your fledging biker. Then, as she gets more comfortable on the bike, increasingly angle the wheels off the ground. This allows the bike to tilt to the side and helps your child learn how to balance.

Time to go solo. Once you think your kid has his balance and braking skills down, it's time to take off the training wheels and let him go solo. This can be a big step, so be empathetic but firm. Find a flat surface with plenty of room for riding. An empty parking lot is good place. Make sure your child is wearing a helmet. You want to protect that soft noggin of his. Get him on the bike and hold the back of the bike seat. Tell him to start pedaling. Run alongside while holding the back of the seat. Offer some encouraging words and tell him to keep looking forward. When you feel like he has his balance, let go of the bike's seat. To avoid a possible freak-out and an ensuing spill, don't tell him you're letting go. **(FIGURE 5.6)**

FIGURE 5.6 Make sure your child is wearing a helmet. Get him on the bike and hold the back of the bike seat. Tell him to start pedaling. Run alongside while holding the back of the seat.

Put on the brakes. Your kid might not have any problems with starting, but she might have some trouble stopping by herself. When you're first teaching your kid to ride, it's a good idea to stay close to her side in case she needs some help stopping. Eventually, though, it's just something she has to learn, even if this means falling.

Administer first aid as needed. If your kid crashes and burns after you let go, first stifle any urge to laugh out loud. Then check to make sure he's not injured. If you don't see any protruding bones or road rash, dust off his behind and get him back on the bike. If he garnered some war wounds, take him inside and patch him up.

Get 'em back on the horse. It's important to encourage your kid to get right back on the bike; allowing her to stew on her crash will only increase her trepidation about making another ride. Repeat that sage line from *Batman*: "Why do we fall, Master [insert child's name here]?

So we can learn to pick ourselves up." After you get your kid pumped, repeat the process above until she can ride solo.

If your son or daughter still refuses to get back in the saddle, have them watch some inspiring movies that show the dazzling possibilities a bike can open up to a kid, such as *E.T.: The Extra-Terrestrial* or *The Goonies*. They'll be back on their bike and hunting for buried treasure in no time.

MANLY ADVICE

BRAID YOUR DAUGHTER'S HAIR

Mom's out of town or maybe you're a single dad. What are you going to do when your daughter asks you to braid her hair? Braiding looks difficult, but once you do it a few times you'll be a pro. Here's how it's done.

1. Make sure her hair is brushed out. You don't want any tangles in her hair or braiding will be next to impossible. Give it a few brushes to straighten it out.
2. Divide her hair into three even sections.
3. Take the right section and cross it over the center section.
4. Take the left section and cross it over the center section (which was formerly the right section). **(FIGURE 5.7)**
5. Take the new right section and cross it over the center section. (You are always crossing a side piece over the middle, just alternating sides.) **(FIGURE 5.8)**
6. Repeat until you get a couple of inches from the end of your daughter's hair. You can tighten the braid by pulling the center section in a horizontal line as you pull it to the right or left. **(FIGURE 5.9)**

7. Secure the end of the braid with a hair elastic.

You can do braided pigtails the same way. Just divide her hair into two even halves. Start on the right half and divide it into three even sections. Braid. Repeat on the left side.

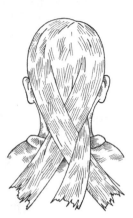
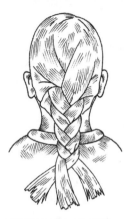

FIGURE 5.7 Take the left section and cross it over the center section.

FIGURE 5.8 Take the new right section and cross it over the center section.

FIGURE 5.9 Repeat until you get a couple of inches from the end of the hair.

◄ ENTERTAIN THE KIDS ►

It's the eternal refrain of kids everywhere: "We're bored!" When you hear this plaintive cry, you can do as our moms did and suggest the completion of a chore as the solution to the problem. Or you can be the cool dad and corral the kids into doing a fun activity. The following are three activities that cost little to no money, will unhook your children's brains from Playstation's deeply embedded tethers and will further cement your awesome dad status. Of course, you may have to learn or brush up on these skills yourself, so here's your chance.

HOW TO SKIP A STONE

Taking your kids to a nearby pond is a surefire way to cure their cabin fever. A pond provides a myriad of free activities: watching the wildlife, feeding the ducks and, of course, skipping stones. Skipping stones is a great way to bond with your kids. You can talk about life while you're throwing stones across the water. If it's been awhile since you've skipped a stone or if you never have, read through the following steps.

Pick the right stone. The key to successful stone skipping is the stone. Ideally it should be flat, of uniform thickness—or thinness—and about the size of your palm. It should weigh about as much as a tennis ball or whatever you can comfortably throw. Too heavy and your projectile won't launch aerodynamically; too light and it'll be like heaving a sponge.

Hold the stone between your thumb and middle finger, with your thumb on top, and your index finger hooked along the edge.

Stand facing the water at a slight angle. With the rock in your hand, pull your arm back like you're going to throw a sidearm pitch. As you

FIGURE 5.10 Stand facing the water at a slight angle. With the rock in your hand, pull your arm back. As you throw the rock, cock your wrist back. Right before you release the stone, give your wrist a quick flick.

throw the rock, cock your wrist back. Right before you release the stone, give your wrist a quick flick. This will create the spin needed for the stone to skip across the water. Also, the lower your arm is when you release the stone, the better the skip you'll get. **(FIGURE 5.10)**

Throw out and down at the same time. The stone should hit the water as parallel to the surface as possible. If you want to get the most skips, the stone should enter the water at a 10 degree angle. Scientists in 2002 (evidently taking a break from designing rockets for a groundbreaking study on stone skipping) were able to calculate this as the perfect angle for maximizing skips.

Try throwing as fast as you can—quickness is the key. Release the stone with a sharp wrist snap to give it some spin; then watch it skip.

If your kid (or you) can't get a skip the first few tries, keep at it. Stone skipping, like all things in life, takes practice. Use the time together to talk and connect.

How to Fold a Paper Airplane

When it comes to teaching your kids how to fold a paper airplane, you can get fancy with complex origami-like folds, but simple is usually better. Below is a time-tested paper airplane design that flies straight for long distances.

1. Get a piece of rectangular paper: notebook paper, printer paper, any paper will do. Printer paper is the best because it has an ideal weight for paper airplanes.
2. Fold the paper in half lengthwise. Precision is key, so make sure the edges line up. Once you make the initial crease, go back over it again with your thumb to make it sharper.
3. Open the paper back up. Take the right top corner and fold it down toward the crease. You should have a triangular flap. Again, make sure the edges line up.

4. Repeat with the other side. Fold the left top corner down toward the crease.

5. You will now repeat steps 3 and 4. Take the right diagonal edge of your triangle and fold it down to the original crease. Line up the edges and make a sharp crease.

6. Repeat on the other side. Fold the left diagonal edge into the crease.

7. Fold it in half along the original crease. It should now look somewhat like a right triangle.

8. Take one of the diagonal edges and fold it down toward the original crease.

9. Repeat on the other side.

10. On the bottom of the plane, make a small ½-inch rip about 5 inches from the nose. Make another tear ½ inch behind the first rip. This should create a small tab. Fold it up. This will hold the two sides of the plane together while in flight. You're now ready to engage in high-flying adventures with your kiddos. Have fun.

HOW TO MAKE AND FLY A KITE

Kids love flying kites, and it's even more fun for them when they get to make the kite themselves. You'll enjoy it more too, knowing that instead of a forty dollar kite stuck in that tree it's just a garbage bag and some sticks.

Materials you'll need:

- two wooden sticks (One needs to be 35 inches, the other needs to be 40 inches. They must be light enough to go airborne but sturdy enough not to break in flight. Bamboo or thin wooden dowels that are ¼-inch in diameter work best.)
- plastic garbage bag
- masking tape

- garden twine
- craft knife

How to build it:

1. Start building the frame by forming a cross with the dowels. Lay the 35-inch stick across the 40-inch stick, about 9 inches from the top of the 40 incher. Tie the two sticks together with some twine. Secure it further by adding some masking tape.

2. Place a small notch at the end of each stick with the craft knife. The notches will hold the string that will go around the kite frame.

3. Take your twine, and starting at the bottom, thread the twine through each notch all the way around. Repeat this step, being sure that the string is kept taut. Finish at the bottom and tie a knot. Place masking tape over each stick end. This will ensure that the string won't pop out of the notches. You've made the kite frame.

4. Cut open the garbage bag and lay it flat on the table. Lay the kite frame on the bag. Cut around the kite frame on the plastic bag, adding an extra inch all the way around so that you can fold it over and eventually tape it to the string frame. This is your kite sail.

5. Fold the edges of the trash bag kite sail over the string frame and tape down with masking tape.

6. Add a tail. Tails have both a practical and aesthetic function. Their most important function is that they keep the kite flying upright. They also make the kite look cool. You can get creative with your kite tail. Add some crepe paper streamers or just cut a 6-foot-long piece of twine and add some short cloth strips down the length of it. Add the tail to the bottom of the kite.

7. Now it's time to make the bridle. Cut a piece of twine about 5 feet long. Poke a hole through the front of the sail at the point where

the two sticks of the frame meet. Thread one end of the twine through the hole, and tie it to the point where the two sticks of the frame meet. Poke another hole through the front of the sail about an inch from the bottom of the kite. Thread the other end of the twine through that hole and tie it to the stick.

8. Make a bridle loop by taking about 8 inches of string and forming a loop. Tie off the end of the loop with a simple overhand knot. Cut off any excess string.

9. Attach the bridle loop to the middle of the bridle string. This can be done with a simple slipknot over the bridle string.

10. Take the end of the string on the twine spool and attach it to the bridle loop by tying a simple overhand knot. This is your fly string.

Next week: duplicating Ben Franklin's experiment with electricity.

⊰ HAVE "THE TALK" WITH YOUR KIDS ⊱

The Talk. The Birds and the Bees. Most men don't look forward to discussing sex with their children. But in this oversexed society where sexual images are just a mouse click or a channel flip away, it's important that you discuss the subject with your kids. Don't let late night TV or kids at school teach your kids about sex. Be a man and take charge of this important part of your child's education and development.

Have more than just one talk. The Talk should actually be a series of conversations you have with your kiddos throughout childhood. So don't put pressure on yourself to have one talk. There's usually no need to sit them down formally for a lecture. Just naturally share your advice when the topic comes up in conversations. Start talking about sex early, and keep the conversation going throughout childhood and their teenage years.

Use age-appropriate information. When your toddler asks where babies come from, there's no need to get into the details about intercourse, much less condoms and date rape. As they get older, give them more information that is relevant to them. One way to find out what type of information you should give them is to answer your kids' questions with a question. If your eight year old asks you, "What's sex?" ask them, "What do you know about it?" Based on their response, you'll know how to respond.

Take the initiative. Don't wait for your kids to bring up the subject. Be a man and find opportunities to educate your kids about sex.

Make your values about sexuality clear. Different families will have different values about sex. Some will have a strict abstinence approach, while others would rather have their kids practice safe sex. Make your values about sex clear to your kids so there isn't any confusion down the road.

Know your facts. Read up on the subject so that when your kid starts asking questions you'll have the correct answers. If your kid asks you a question that you don't know the answer to, don't make up an answer. That will only cause confusion later on. There are plenty of books out there that discuss sexuality and how to talk about it with your children. Read up on them.

Don't hide the fact that Mom and Dad have sex. While no kid wants to think about their parents doing the deed, you shouldn't pretend like you and your wife took vows of chastity at the altar. While you need not share private or explicit examples from your marital sex life, it's okay to reveal that you're drawing from experience when answering questions. It's important to convey to your kids that sex is a natural and healthy part of a committed relationship, not something yucky or embarrassing.

Be open to questions. Let your kids know that you're always open to questions. Tell them this explicitly and repeatedly. It's better they come to you then find out from a friend on the playground or the Internet.

Relax. Kids can smell fear. If they see that you're uncomfortable talking about sex, they'll get the idea that sex is this bad thing that shouldn't be discussed or they'll go to a source who doesn't break out in cold sweats at the mere mention of the word vagina. Man up by staying calm and collected.

GIVE YOUR SON A RITE OF PASSAGE

When it comes to the journey into adulthood, girls seem to mature faster and make a smoother transition than boys do. Without something to propel them out of it, male adolescence often extends into a guy's twenties, thirties, and in some especially sad cases, even further.

Ancient cultures didn't have to worry too much about men-children loafing around the village mooching off their parents, partly because they had ceremonial rites of passage that served as a clear demarcation between childhood and manhood. These rites of passage were elaborate occasions, celebrated by a young man's entire village and used to initiate a boy into the art of manliness.

Today such rites of passage are unfortunately almost extinct, and boys lack clear markers and helpful mentors on their journey to becoming a man. If you ask them when the transition occurs, you will get a variety of answers: when you get a car, when you graduate college, when you get a real job, when you get married, when you switch from Honey Nut to regular Cheerios, and so on. The problem with many of these traditional rites of passage is that they have been put off further and further in a young man's life. As traditional rites of passage have become fuzzier, young men are plagued with a sense of being adrift.

Of course the process of becoming a man, ceremony or not, does not happen in a single moment. But rites of passage are important in delineating when a boy should start thinking of himself as a man and shouldering the responsibilities of manhood. Lacking these important markers, many young men today belabor their childhood, never sure of when they've manned up. A father can help his son avoid this limbo by creating for him meaningful transition points on his passage into manhood.

MANLY ADVICE

WHEN SHOULD THE RITE OF PASSAGE OCCUR?

Before deciding what the rite of passage will be, you'll first need to decide at what age your son should take part in it. A good time to take your son through a rite of passage into manhood is after he graduates high school. By then, he's about eighteen years old, the age at which society legally deems him an adult. Also, he's about to begin a new chapter in his life. A rite of passage will help him navigate the new path he'll forge for himself.

CREATING A RITE OF PASSAGE FOR YOUR SON

While the whole village will no longer turn out for your son's rite of passage, a family is a very small community unto itself, and parents may create unique familial ceremonies in which their sons are inducted into manhood. The options for such a ceremony are limited only by your creativity. Consider the following:

Enroll your son in Boy Scouts. This is the easiest option. The Scouts have built in "rites of passage" that increase boys' skills, responsibilities and feelings of competence. You can enhance the experience by being a Scout Leader and encouraging your boy to make it to Eagle Scout. **(FIGURE 5.11)**

Draw up a list of tasks your son must learn to perform himself.
If you don't want the structure of the Scouts, you can create your own
goals for your son to achieve. When he has mastered all of these skills,
throw him a celebration in which you present him with a medallion of
some sort to commemorate the occasion.

Increase the significance of religious ceremonies. Religious ceremonies are some of the few rites of passage which are still widely recognized. Yet these ceremonies can either be a big deal, an occasion in
which a boy truly feels like he is transitioning into manhood, or they can
be just another thing he is supposed to do. A dad can make sure it's the
former by impressing upon his son the importance and solemnity of the
occasion. As the time for the ceremony draws closer, schedule weekly
events in which you discuss the principles of your faith, your personal
views on weighty matters and your advice on being a man of faith.

FIGURE 5.11 Enroll your son in Boy Scouts. You can enhance the experience by being a Scout
Leader and encouraging your boy to make it to Eagle Scout.

Take your son on a long backpacking trip. After a series of father/son camping trips, plan an excursion in which your son is responsible for all the necessary duties: making the fire, setting up camp, navigating, cooking food, etc. Along the way, impart all the manly wisdom you have gleaned from life experience.

Send your son on an excursion. A true rite of passage requires a period of separation from one's former life. So consider sending your son on a service trip to a foreign country or on a trip guided by an organization like Outward Bound.

Whichever avenue you choose, the important thing is to imbue the process with great significance. Don't be cheesy about it, be sincere. And treat your son differently when the process is complete, giving him both greater respect and greater responsibility.

CHAPTER SIX

THE OUTDOORSMAN

"Crossing a bare common, in snow puddles, at twilight, under a clouded sky, without having in my thoughts any occurrence of special good fortune, I have enjoyed a perfect exhilaration. ... In the woods too, a man casts off his years. ... In the woods, is perpetual youth."

—RALPH WALDO EMERSON

Many men today feel inexplicably restless, unfulfilled and depressed. They seek all the things society tells them will heal their man spirit: carefully watching their diet, taking supplements, exercising and visiting a shrink. And yet they find no relief. Why? They're skipping out on perhaps the most crucial element in maintaining their manly vigor: spending time in the great outdoors.

Great men from Theodore Roosevelt to Ralph Waldo Emerson loved to tear out into nature. Yet today's men see activities like hiking, fishing, hunting and camping as hobbies to be enjoyed by some and not by others. Such pursuits have become just another recreational opportunity: you can take it or leave it.

But spending time in the outdoors is essential for every man. It's not an extracurricular activity; it's a vital part of nourishing the whole man. The wild will strip off the stale, sissified patina that civilization has covered you in and renew your soul in four crucial ways.

1. Nature gives you a chance for unstructured exploration. Most men's lives are tightly scheduled and routine. Wake up, shower, commute, work, home, sleep. Each day you drive the same route, sit in the same cubicle and sleep in the same bed. Yet within each man is a strong urge to set out and explore, to start out a day with only the faintest outline of an agenda and to discover things never before seen. Scrambling over rocks, hiking up mountains and fording streams will make you feel like a kid again.

2. Nature gets you in touch with the basic elements and your primal self. The modern man is subject to all sorts of rules, expectations and constraints. Buttoned up and buried in paperwork, he must act polite, follow the traffic laws and refrain from throttling the jerk who prolongs company meetings with asinine questions. His spirit is constantly hemmed in. And everything modern man touches, lives in and uses has been modified from its original form: sanded, molded and packaged for consumption. Almost every sound he hears, from the car engine to the ringing cell phone, originates from an artificial source. It's enough to render every man with a mild form of insanity.

While every man should strive to be well mannered, his primal side should not be entirely neglected. Your wild man spirit must be set free from time to time. You must periodically tear yourself away from civilization and interact with things in their natural state. Touch real dirt, sit by a real fire, sharpen real wood and listen to the pure sounds of running streams and the wind in the trees.

3. Nature gives you space to think and puts your problems in perspective. In the cities and suburbs, it's easy to lose track of what is truly important. The world begins to seem as if it really does revolve around your tiny world, a world with few truly quiet moments. In the car you are listening to music or talk radio, at work you're focused on the task at hand and when you get home you turn on the TV and zone out. Getting lost in nature allows quiet unstructured space in which to sort out your problems, think through what's been going on in your life and plan goals for the future. Under the stars and beneath the trees, it's easier to see what really matters. Mountain peaks, rolling rivers and radiant sunsets will make you and your problems seem properly small.

4. Nature invigorates your body. Every now and again men must tear themselves away from the clogged air of the streets and the recycled air of corporate buildings. Your lungs yearn to breathe the fresh air of the forests and mountains. Hiking will invigorate your body. While all exercise is beneficial in alleviating depression and stress, outdoor exercise is particularly useful. The sunlight, physical activity and inspiring scenery will combine to rejuvenate your spirit and leave you ready to once more take on the world.

What follows are a few suggestions and tips as you begin to reconnect with the outdoors and restore your manly vigor.

"Truly it may be said that the outside of a mountain is good for the inside of a man."

—GEORGE WHERRY

So we've established that spending time in the great outdoors should be an essential part of every man's life. Perhaps it's an idea that's crossed your mind before, but you simply couldn't find the time or motivation to follow up on it. You're not alone. According to a recent study, Americans are spending 25 percent less time in the outdoors than they did just two decades ago. People are glued to their television and computer screens. Planning and executing a camping trip feels like too big of a hassle.

Yet it always seems more troublesome in your BRAIN-CANISTER than it turns out to be. The great thing about camping is that it is the most economical and easy way to get away from it all. And there are several things you can do to make camping trips simpler and consequently more frequent. Here are five ways to streamline your camping trip and keep it hassle free.

1. Find your campsite online. One of the reasons people don't camp more frequently is that they don't know where to go. Thankfully the Internet has made finding a camping spot far easier. All states operate websites about their state parks. Click on a park that sparks your interest and see what it offers. Your choice of park will be based on your personal desires. Some parks offer amenities like toilets, water pumps and showers, while others are more remote and rustic. Some parks sit on a lake and are known for their fishing but lack hiking trails. Pick a park that offers the kind of setting and activities you are looking for.

Also, consider the distance. You don't want the tiredness that results from long drives to cancel out the rejuvenation camping affords. For a weekend getaway, don't travel much farther than three hours from your home.

If you are having trouble picking a park, visit a local camping and outdoor supply store. Generally the employees there are outdoor enthusiasts and will be able to give you some advice.

2. Reserve your campsite before leaving. This is recommended for state parks, and essential if you'll be visiting a popular national park like Yosemite. Popular parks fill up fast. The last thing you want to do is drive for several hours only to find that there are no available campsites. Many state park websites allow you to book online. If not, all you have to do is call ahead.

3. Keep most of your camping stuff in one big storage tub. Part of the hassle of putting a camping trip together is having to rummage through the attic and make last-minute runs to the store to gather all the supplies you'll need. To avoid this annoyance, simply keep most of your camping equipment in a big plastic storage tub. Once you have your camping tub loaded up, whenever the urge to tear out into the woods strikes, you can simply grab it and go. Specific supplies may vary according to what kind of camping you'll be doing, where you're going and what season it is. But this list covers the basics:

- tent
- sleeping bags
- sleeping pads
- first aid kit
- lantern
- flashlight
- extra batteries
- small whisk broom
- tarp
- matches
- bug repellent
- trash bags

- cooking supplies (this can be skipped, see #5 below)
- water jug

4. Create a permanent checklist that you can consult before each trip. This list is for the things that won't fit in a tub or need to be packed right before the trip, and might include:

- sunscreen
- pocketknife
- camp or lawn chairs
- clothes
- food
- firewood (if you don't think there will be enough at your campsite to gather)
- toothbrush
- cooler

5. Avoid cooking elaborate meals. Admittedly one of the joys of camping is cooking and eating delicious campfire chow. But cooking supplies can add a dozen or more things to your list of supplies in addition to the hassle of cleaning. So save camp cooking for a weeklong trip. If you just want to get away for the weekend, plan two meals that involve zero cookware and no cleanup. Here is the menu we always use when we go away for a Friday afternoon to Sunday afternoon trip:

Friday night meal: Foil dinners. Wrap hamburger meat, canned mixed vegetables, cream of mushroom soup and spices in a foil pouch, and you're good to go. Put together the foil dinner before leaving and place in a cooler. To cook, simply place the foil packet on the coals of the fire. The only thing you need is a fork.

Saturday night meal: Hot dogs. No tools needed here. Simply roast your dog on a stick. Few things are easier to prepare and taste better than campfire weenies.

For dessert on both nights, we eat s'mores. And the rest of the time we just snack on energy bars, trail mix and chips. No pots, no pans, no cleanup.

As an alternative to this meal plan, consider freeze-dried or dehydrated camp food. The food is lightweight and eminently packable. And all you need to bring is a pot to boil the water. For more hassle-free cooking ideas, see "Five Foods You Can Cook on a Stick" on page 193.

⊰ SET UP CAMP ⊱

When you're out in the wild, your campsite will be your home away from home. Taking care to properly set up your outdoor abode will greatly enhance the comfort and enjoyment of your camping trip.

SELECT A CAMPSITE

"But the place which you have selected for your camp, though never so rough and grim, begins at once to have its attractions, and becomes a very centre of civilization to you: Home is home, be it never so homely."

—HENRY DAVID THOREAU

This is the most important decision you'll make when striking camp. When choosing a campsite, you should take into account a couple of factors. First, think about safety. Don't camp in low-lying or marshy areas that are prone to flooding and stay away from high areas, like mountain tops, that are targets for lightning. Don't camp beneath large tree branches. Dead branches, known as "widow makers," can snap, fall and flatten you into a mancake.

Second, look for a campsite near a water source. Many campsites offer running water which you can use for drinking, cooking and bathing. If you plan on taking water from rivers or lakes, make sure you purify it before drinking. This can be done by boiling, filtering or using purification tablets.

PITCH YOUR TENT

After you've selected your site, it's time to set up your temporary home. How you'll pitch a tent will vary depending on the kind of tent it is. So see your owner's manual for exact details. What follows are some general guidelines for pitching success.

Lay the tarp. It's a good idea to bring a tarp as a ground cover for your tent. If it rains, the bottom of your tent will be kept dry. Even if it doesn't rain, the tarp prevents moisture from the morning dew from soaking through the floor of the tent.

Arrange the tent. Lay the tent over the tarp. If there's a light breeze, arrange the tent to face the wind. This will help increase ventilation and reduce condensation in your tent.

FIGURE 6.1 After you've set up your tent, make sure to put on the rain fly. Even if it doesn't rain, the fly will keep out any dew that might settle on the roof of your tent.

If the wind is blowing strongly, pitch the tent to face downwind. Otherwise, when you open the tent door, the tent will inflate like a balloon and rain can blow in.

Stake the corners. After you have rolled out the tent on top of the tarp, it's a good idea to stake down the corners of the tent. You'll especially want to do this if it's windy; you don't want your nylon hut to blow away.

Pitch the tent. Most tents are pretty easy to put up these days. It's just a matter of threading the right poles through the right loops. After you've set up you tent, make sure to put on the rain fly. Even if it doesn't rain, the fly will keep out any dew that might settle on the roof of your tent. **(FIGURE 6.1)**

MAKE A LATRINE

If you're camping in an area without available restroom facilities, you'll need to create a latrine. Having a latrine helps prevent sickness and reduces your impact on the land. The easiest type of outdoor john to build is the trench latrine.

With a shovel, dig a shallow trench that's about a foot wide and 3 to 4 feet long. Don't make the trench deeper than the ground soil. Every time nature calls, "flush" your latrine by sprinkling a layer of dirt over your waste. This will keep flies from using your trench as a gourmet restaurant and will reduce odors so that all you smell are the pine trees and wildflowers.

◄ MAN AND FIRE ►

"To poke a wood fire is more solid enjoyment than almost anything else in the world."

—CHARLES DUDLEY WARNER

There is a primal link between man and fire. For ancient man, fire provided warmth, protection from wild animals, light in pitch-black nights and a place to cook food. While fire is no longer vital to most men's existence, it still has a magnetic power that attracts us. The flames of fire can inspire legendary stories, generate uplifting discussion, build camaraderie among the men circled around them and create a romantic setting for cuddling up to your gal. No camping trip is complete without one. For these reasons, and many more, every man should know how to start a great fire and be well practiced in doing so.

Whether you create your flame using one of the matchless methods or just a Bic lighter, you need to know how to take your burning tinder nest and transform it into a roaring campfire you can be proud of. Here's how:

CREATE YOUR FIRE BED

When building a fire, always think about safety first. You don't want to be that guy who starts a raging wildfire in a national park. If your camping site has a designated fire area, use it. If you're camping in a more rugged area that lacks fire sites, you'll need to make your own. Select a site away from trees, bushes and other plant material. Your fire bed should be made on bare earth, not grass. If you can't find a bare area, make your own by digging and raking away plant material, taking particular care in clearing away all dry (and thus highly flammable) grass, branches and bark.

After you've cleared the area, it's time to make your bed. Gather dirt and place it in the center of your cleared area. Form the dirt into a platform that's about 3 to 4 inches thick.

GATHER YOUR WOOD

You'll need three basic types of materials to build your roaring campfire: tinder, kindling and fuel wood.

Tinder. Every good campfire starts with good tinder. Tinder catches fire easily but burns fast. Material like dry leaves, dry bark, wood shavings, dry grass and some fluffy funguses make for good tinder. If you're a smart camper, you'll bring your own tinder in the form of dryer lint. Bringing your own lint is especially important when everything outside is wet. Wet tinder does not catch on fire.

Kindling. You'll need something with more substance than tinder to keep your flame going. You can't move directly to big logs. You'll end up smothering your little flame. That's where kindling comes in. Kindling usually consists of small twigs and branches. Go for something that's about the width of a pencil. Like tinder, kindling needs to be dry or it won't burn easily. If all you have are wet twigs and branches, try whittling away the damp bark with your pocketknife.

Fuel wood. Fuel wood is what keeps your fire hot and burning. Contrary to popular belief, fuel wood doesn't have to look like the huge logs you use in a fireplace. If you go too big, it's going to take a long time for the wood to catch fire. Look for branches that are about as wide as your wrist or your forearm.

When gathering wood for a fire, collect wood that snaps and breaks easily. Dry wood burns the best. If your wood bends, it's too wet or green. If you try to make a fire with this sort of wood, you'll just get a lot of smoke. Unlike tinder and kindling, fuel wood can be a little damp. The fire will dry it out. But it's definitely not ideal.

LAY YOUR FIRE

There are several ways to lay your fire. The teepee is probably the most effective:

1. Place your tinder bundle in the middle of your campfire site.
2. Above your tinder bundle, form a teepee with some kindling. Leave an opening in your teepee on the side the wind is blowing

against. This will ensure that your fire gets the air it needs to blow the flames onto the kindling. **(FIGURE 6.2)**

3. Continue adding kindling to the teepee, working your way up to pencil-sized twigs.

4. Create a larger teepee structure around your kindling teepee with your fuel wood.

5. Place a match under your tinder. Because this lay directs the flame up, the flame should rise to the kindling and then on to the fuel wood.

6. The teepee structure will eventually fall, and at this point you can simply add some fuel logs to the fire.

FIGURE 6.2 Above your tinder bundle, form a teepee with some kindling. Leave an opening in your teepee on the side the wind is blowing against to ensure that your fire gets the air it needs.

FIVE WAYS TO START A FIRE WITHOUT MATCHES

Anybody can light a Duraflame log with some matches or a lighter. A manly man knows how to create fire in the absence of either. Knowing how to make fire without matches is an essential survival skill. Maybe your single-engine plane goes down while you're flying over the Alaskan wilderness, like the kid in *Hatchet*. Or perhaps you're out camping and you lose your backpack in a tussle with a bear. Whether or not you ever need to call upon these skills, it's just damn cool to know you can start a fire, whenever and wherever you are. Few skill sets are as deeply satisfying to possess.

FRICTION-BASED FIRE-MAKING METHODS

Friction-based fire making is not for the faint of heart. It's arguably the most difficult of all the non-match methods. There are different techniques you can use to make a fire with friction, but the most important factor is the type of wood you use for the fire board and spindle.

The spindle is the stick you'll spin to create friction between it and the fire board. If you create enough friction between the spindle and the fire board, you'll produce an ember that can be used to create a fire. Cottonwood, juniper, aspen, willow, cedar, cypress and walnut make the best woods for fire board and spindle sets.

Before you can use wood to start a friction-based fire, the wood must be bone dry. If the wood isn't dry, you'll have to dry it out first.

If you have the patience and dedication to turn elbow grease into embers, here are two friction-based fire-making methods with which to try your hand.

Fire Plough

1. Prepare your fire board. Cut a groove in the fire board. This will be your track for the spindle.

2. Rub! Take the tip of your spindle and place it in the groove of your fire board. Start rubbing the tip of the spindle up and down the groove.

3. Start a fire. Have your tinder nest at the end of the fire board, so that you'll plow embers into it as you're rubbing. Once you catch one, blow the nest gently and get that fire going.

Bow Drill

The bow drill is probably the most effective friction-based method to use because it's easier to maintain the speed and pressure you need to create enough friction to start a fire. In addition to the spindle and fire board, you'll also need a socket and a bow.

1. Get a socket. The socket is used to put pressure on the other end of the spindle as you're rotating it with the bow. The socket can be a stone or another piece of wood. If you use another piece of wood, try to find a harder piece than what you're using for the spindle. Woods with sap and oil are good as they create a lubricant between the spindle and the socket.

2. Make your bow. The bow should be about as long as your arm. Use a flexible piece of wood that has a slight curve. The string of the bow can be anything. A shoelace, rope or strip of rawhide works great. Just find something that won't break. String up your bow, and you're ready to begin.

FIGURE 6.3 Using your bow, start sawing back and forth. The spindle should be rotating quickly. Go at it until you create an ember.

3. Prepare the fire board. Cut a V-shaped notch and create a depression adjacent to it in the fire board. Underneath the notch, place your tinder.

4. String up the spindle. Catch the spindle in a loop of the bow string. Place one end of the spindle in the fire board and apply pressure on the other end with your socket.

5. Start sawing. Using your bow, start sawing back and forth. You've basically created a rudimentary mechanical drill. The spindle should be rotating quickly. Go at it FULL CHISEL until you create an ember. (FIGURE 6.3)

6. Make your fire. Drop the ember into the tinder nest and blow on it gently. You've got yourself a fire.

FLINT AND STEEL METHOD

This is an old standby. It's always a good idea to carry around a flint and steel set on camping trips. In wet conditions, matches will be rendered useless, but flint and steel will still create a spark. You should ideally bring along a char cloth as well. The char cloth catches the spark and keeps it smoldering, without bursting into flames. If you don't have a char cloth, a piece of fungus or birch will do.

If you're caught without a flint and steel set, you can always improvise by using quartzite and the steel blade of your pocketknife.

1. Grip the flint (or quartzite) and char cloth. Take hold of the piece of rock between your thumb and forefinger. Make sure an edge is hanging out about 2 or 3 inches. Grasp the char cloth between your thumb and the flint.

2. Strike! Grasp the back of the steel striker or use the back of your knife blade. Strike the steel against the flint several times. Sparks from the steel will fly off and land on the char cloth, and it will begin to burn.

3. Start a fire. Fold your char cloth into the tinder nest and gently blow on it to start a flame.

Lens-Based Method

Using a lens to start a fire is an easy matchless method. Any boy who has melted green plastic army men with a magnifying glass will know how to do this. If you have by chance never played God with your action figures, here's how to do it.

To create a fire, all you need is some sort of lens to focus sunlight on a specific spot. A magnifying glass, eyeglasses (the concave lenses that correct nearsightedness won't work, only those for reading glasses or farsightedness will do), or binocular lenses are all effective. If you add some water to the lens, you can intensify the beam.

1. Angle the lens. Angle it toward the sun in order to focus the beam into as small an area as possible. **(FIGURE 6.4)**

FIGURE 6.4 Angle the lens toward the sun in order to focus the beam into as small an area as possible.

CHAPTER SIX

2. Prepare the tinder. Put your tinder nest under this spot and you'll soon have yourself a fire.

The only drawback to the lens-based method is that it only works when you have sun. So if it's nighttime or overcast, you won't have any luck.

STEEL WOOL AND BATTERIES METHOD

It's hard to imagine a situation where you won't have matches, but you will have batteries and steel wool. But hey, you never know, just ask MacGyver. And it's quite easy and fun to try at home.

1. Stretch out the steel wool. You want it to be about 6 inches long and ½ inch wide.

2. Rub the battery on the steel wool. Hold the steel wool in one hand and the battery in the other. Any battery will do, but nine-volt batteries work best. Rub the battery's contacts on the wool. The wool will begin to glow and burn. Gently blow on it.

Transfer the burning wool to your tinder nest. The wool's flame will extinguish quickly, so don't waste any time.

MANLY ADVICE

FIVE FOODS YOU CAN COOK ON A STICK

As mentioned, the easiest way to streamline your camping trip is to eat meals that don't require any cookware, preparation or cleanup. Enter stick cooking. With only the blazing fire you just made, simple provisions and a rod of wood, you can make a complete meal. And nothing tastes better or feels more satisfyingly primal than filling your DUMPLING-DEPOT with food fresh from the flames.

CHOOSING YOUR STICK

It's the only cooking utensil you'll be employing, so make it a good one. Find a stick that is sufficiently long to enable you to sit far enough from the fire so you don't get scorched as you cook, and sturdy enough that your stick won't droop and release its precious cargo into the fire. After you choose your stick, whittle off the bark on the end so you have a smooth, clean area with which to spear your food.

YOUR GOURMET STICK MENU

1. Meat of any sort. While the hot dog's tubelike shape clearly cries out to be impaled, any meat you can put a stick through can be cooked over a fire. Go ahead and spear yourself a steak, pork chop or chicken breast. Extra man points if you kill your own meat in the wild. You may need to make the initial hole with your knife and then thread your stick through. And make sure your stick is sufficiently strong; losing a hot dog to the fire gods is one thing, having the flames consume your juicy tenderloin quite another.

2. Marshmallow. This item surely needs little explanation. It constitutes the finest stick dessert available to man. And there is only one way to consume this delicacy: golden brown and slightly crisp on the outside, hot and gooey on the inside. The barbarous man will stick his marshmallow directly in the fire, quickly charring the marshmallow in a crude flameout. The civilized outdoorsman, understanding well the delicate nature of the marshmallow, is willing to patiently roast it, turning it constantly until it is golden brown and ready to be sacrificed on a graham cracker altar.

3. Biscuits. Not enough men know that delicious biscuits can be made with only a stick and a fire. Start with a can of refrigerated biscuit dough. Break off one of the biscuits and if needed, flatten it until it's about ¾ inch in thickness. Wrap it around the end of stick, firmly pinching the sides together. Slowly roast it like a marshmallow, turning constantly until golden brown. When done, eat it plain or place sausage, butter or jam inside. You can also take biscuit dough and wrap it around a hot dog for a pig in a blanket on a stick.

4. Grilled cheese. Grilled cheese is the ultimate comfort food, so why not have Mother Nature help whip one up while out in the woods? First, find two forked sticks. The forks must be wide enough and long enough to be able to securely balance a piece of bread. Butter two slices of bread and rest one on top of the first stick. Add a couple of slices of cheese and cover them with the other slice of bread. Toast the sandwich. When the bottom slice is brown, take your second stick and lay it on top of the sandwich. Carefully flip over the sandwich, and toast the other side.

5. Egg. There are more ways to cook an egg than you can shake a stick at, and to this list we can add a stick itself. Using the point of your pocketknife, very gently make two small holes on both tips of the egg. Carefully thread a very thin stick through the hole on the egg's wider end and out the hole on the narrower end. Keeping the egg horizontal, roast it over the coals. When the egg becomes difficult to pull off the stick and egg white ceases to leak from the holes, it's done and ready to be eaten.

Before hot weather women, Al Roker and weather.com, men predicted the weather on their own. Using aches in their bones and clues from Mother Nature, frontiersmen could predict the next day's, or even week's, forecast. When you're out camping and away from your Blackberry, being able to predict the weather like Daniel Boone is a critical and manly skill to possess.

"RED SKY AT NIGHT, SAILORS DELIGHT. RED SKY IN THE MORNING, SAILORS TAKE WARNING."

It turns out Shakespeare, the Bible and skippers the world over were right; this familiar rhyme is actually a fairly accurate way to predict the weather. If the sky at sunset is red, a high-pressure system with dry air is coming in and whipping up dust. The longer red wavelengths of light break through the atmosphere, while shorter wavelengths of color are dissipated. If you see a red sky at sunrise, it means the dry air has already moved past you and a moisture-laden low-pressure system is on its way.

LOOK TO THE CLOUDS

Cirrus clouds. Cirrus clouds are the long, wispy clouds that hang high up in the sky. Low-hanging cirrus clouds that look like a horse's tail mean bad weather is on its way. **(FIGURE 6.5)**

Cumulus clouds. Cumulus clouds are the big puffy clouds that angels use for harp playing and Care Bears employ as cars. If the cumulus clouds are white, like a giant cotton ball, you can expect good weather for the day. If they get darker and more ominous, expect thunder, lightning and a murder at the old inn. **(FIGURE 6.6)**

FIGURE 6.5 Low-hanging cirrus clouds that look like a horse's tail mean bad weather is on its way.

FIGURE 6.6 If the cumulus clouds are white, you can expect good weather for the day. If they get darker and more ominous, expect thunder and lightning.

FIGURE 6.7 Stratus clouds that are hanging medium to high in the sky can mean rain in the next thirty-six hours.

Stratus clouds. Stratus clouds look like a white blanket covering a portion of the sky. Stratus clouds that are hanging medium to high in the sky can mean rain in the next thirty-six hours. **(FIGURE 6.7)**

Clouds on a winter night. If you see clouds on a winter night, you can expect warmer weather.

CHECK OUT THE MOON

A ring around the moon. Cirrostratus clouds can sometimes create the appearance of a ring or halo around the moon. Ice crystals in the clouds refract light and produce this illusion. Cirrostratus clouds often precede a warm front and indicate that rain or snow will fall within thirty-six hours.

Moon in the sky like a big pizza pie. The forecast calls for *amore*.

OBSERVE THE PLANTS

Pinecones. Pinecones will remain closed if humidity is high. High humidity often means precipitation is likely. If the weather is dry, pinecones will open up.

Plants. A plant's leaves will often curl in high humidity, foretelling a chance for rain. Additionally plants release waste in low pressure atmospheres, so if it smells like compost in your neck of the woods, bring a poncho.

OBSERVE ANIMALS

Cows. Cloudy weather apparently makes our bovine friends melancholy. When rain's on the way, they lay down, sulk and read *Catcher in the Rye.*

Birds. If you see birds flying high in the sky, it means clear weather. However, if you see a lot of birds roosting on power lines and trees, this either means they're conspiring against you or falling air pressure and bad weather are on the way. Expect rain and/or a killer seagull attack in the next twelve hours.

Bees. Bees stay near their hive when rain is imminent.

MANLY ADVICE

CLEAN A FISH

There's nothing like fishing to help reconnect you with the rhythms of life. The gurgling of a running stream, the chirping of insects and the rhythmic casting of your rod can all bring you to a Zen-like state. When you catch a fish, your meditative trance is broken with excitement, and you have a choice to make: whether to release the fish or keep it and cook it. If you choose the latter, you're going to have to clean it before it can become your dinner. It takes a little work, but nothing is as satisfying as preparing a meal from something you caught in the wild.

Wash. Before you start slicing up your fish, wash it with some clear running water. You can do this underneath a faucet, but you get more man points for washing the fish in a clear mountain stream.

Cut the fins. Take a knife and cut off the pectoral fins on both sides of the fish.

Scale it. With a dull knife or the back of the sharp knife you used to cut the fins off, scale the fish. This is done by holding the blunt

FIGURE 6.8 Scale the fish by holding the blunt knife at a 90 degree angle to the body of the fish and dragging it across the fish from tail to head.

knife at a 90 degree angle to the body of the fish and dragging it across the fish from tail to head. Continue scraping until the body is smooth. **(FIGURE 6.8)**

Gut it. Make a cut down the middle of the fish's belly from the gills to the anal vent. Holding onto the jaws of the fish, pull the gills and guts from the fish's insides. Make sure everything is cleaned out of it. You may need to get a spoon and scoop out the kidney. It's the dark red line on the backbone of the fish.

Rinse. After you've scraped it clean, give the cavity of the fish a good rinsing.

Remove the dorsal fin. Remove the dorsal fin by cutting both sides of it and removing it with pliers. You can cook the fish whole or you can remove the head and the tail. It comes down to personal preference and whether you mind having your dinner eyeball you.

◄ NAVIGATE WITHOUT A COMPASS ►

"Everybody needs beauty as well as bread, places to play in and pray in where nature may heal and cheer and give strength to the body and soul. Keep close to Nature's heart … and break clear away, once in awhile, and climb a mountain or spend a week in the woods. Wash your spirit clean."

—JOHN MUIR

Before GPS and even before maps and compasses, man was able to navigate his world simply by looking to the sky and his natural surroundings. Sadly, because of a dependence on technology, the ability to navigate without tools has become a forgotten skill. While technology is accurate, it can let you down when you need it most.

Don't be the man who freaks out just because he lost his precious directional gadget. A real man knows how to find his way in the world with only his wits and savvy. Compass? We don't need no stinking compass.

USE THE NORTH STAR TO NAVIGATE

NOTE: The tips below will only work if you're in the Northern Hemisphere.

The North Star, or Polaris, has served as a beacon for generations of lost sailors and explorers. Once you find it, you can easily orient yourself and start heading in the right direction.

To locate Polaris, you must first find the ladle-shaped Big and Little Dipper constellations. Then train your eyes on the star that makes up the lip of the ladle of the Big Dipper. Draw an imaginary line from it to the last, brightest star of the handle of the Little Dipper. This is the North Star. Now with a simple Never Eat Shredded Wheat, you're on your way. **(FIGURE 6.9)**

FIGURE 6.9 Then train your eyes on the star that makes up the lip of the ladle of the Big Dipper. Draw an imaginary line from it to the last, brightest star of the handle of the Little Dipper. This is the North Star.

USE THE SUN TO NAVIGATE

Shadow Stick. Place a stick into the ground and angle it so it points toward the sun. You shouldn't see the stick's shadow at this point. Now wait. Dig for arrowheads or wrestle a grizzly. When the stick casts a shadow that's at least 6 inches long, you'll know it's pointing east. Draw an imaginary perpendicular line across the shadow. That's north and south.

Watch Method. This will only work if you have an analog watch. Your Casio calculator watch unfortunately won't cut it. Also, your watch must be set to standard time, so turn it back if it's on daylight savings time. Take off your watch and hold it level. Grab a short straight twig and place it perpendicular to the watch, lining up the bottom end of the twig with the hour hand. Now move the watch and twig together until the twig's shadow falls along the hour hand. The spot midway between the hour hand and the number twelve on your watch points south.

Finally, forget what you saw in the movies about finding moss on only the north sides of trees. Moss can grow on every side of a tree. Curse that wily moss!

⊲ FOUR KNOTS EVERY MAN SHOULD KNOW ⊳

Whether you're tying down a rain fly on your tent or rescuing your friend from a ravine, knowing a few essential knots will help you get the job done safely and correctly. Unfortunately many men don't know how to tie real knots and end up just looping and weaving rope into a jumbled mess that only appears secure. If you don't want to see your canoe fall off the top of your car as your cruise the interstate, learn to tie knots correctly. To get you started, here's a run down of four basic knots every man should know.

SQUARE KNOT (FIGURE 6.10)

Also known as the "reef knot" to our British friends, the square knot is a good solid general-purpose binding knot. Sailors use it on a boat to tie sails down. You use it everyday when you tie your shoe. The square knot should not be used to tie ropes together. However, if you need to tie something down with a piece of rope, this is a good one to use.

1. Hold one end of each rope in each hand.
2. Take the end in your left hand and cross it over the right end. You should now have an "X."
3. Take that same left end (which is now on your right) and wrap it around the right end. You now have something that kind of resembles a "W."
4. Cross the right end over the left to make a knot. Pull it tightly.

BOWLINE KNOT (FIGURE 6.11)

The bowline knot makes a secure loop at the end of a rope. When there's load on it, it doesn't slip or bind. A bowline is a good knot to use when you want to fasten a mooring line to a post. Because the knot doesn't slip, the bowline can be used to lift a victim who's fallen down a ravine or hole.

1. Form a small loop near the end of the rope.
2. Take the other end of the rope and pull it up through the loop. Pull it through until you form the right size loop for the object that it will be going around.
3. Wrap it around the standing part of the rope.
4. Bring that same end back down through the same loop you came up through. Pull it tight to form a knot.

An easy mnemonic device to remember how to tie this knot is to imagine the end of the rope is a rabbit, the loop is the rabbit hole, and the stand-

FIGURE 6.10 Square knot.

FIGURE 6.11 Bowline knot.

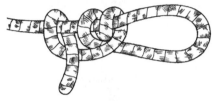

FIGURE 6.12 Taut-line knot.

FIGURE 6.13 Figure eight knot.

ing part of the rope is a tree. The rabbit goes up the hole, around the tree, back down the hole and boom! You've got yourself a bowline.

TAUT-LINE KNOT (FIGURE 6.12)

The taut-line is an adjustable knot that allows you to lengthen or shorten a rope as needed. The taut-line is especially useful in pitching a tent. You can use it to tighten or loosen a tent guy line (the line used to secure a tent or rain fly).

How to tie it:

1. First, pass one end of the rope around a tent stake and bring it back toward the standing part of the rope.
2. Take the end of the rope underneath the long standing length of the rope, and drop it down through the hole between where the rope crosses and the stake.
3. Bring the rope around and drop it again.
4. Bring the end of the rope back to the front of the two loops you just made and form a third loop around the standing part of the rope.

5. Pull the end through the loop you created to the side while making that third loop.

FIGURE EIGHT KNOT (FIGURE 6.13)

The figure eight knot is a stopper knot like the bowline knot. It's an essential knot for mountain and rock climbing. Learn how to tie it correctly or you'll find yourself at the bottom of an icy crevasse and an easy snack for a hungry yeti.

How to tie it:

1. Form a loop with the rope by crossing one end on top of the rope.
2. Bring the right end of the rope around to the left side of the loop.
3. Bring the end of the rope up through the loop.
4. If you've done everything right, the knot should look like a figure eight.

CHAPTER SEVEN

⊰ THE ⊱ LEADER

"A leader is a man who can
adapt principles to circumstances."
—GENERAL GEORGE S. PATTON JR.

We all lead at some point in our lives. We serve as leaders in our jobs, in our communities and in our families. For many, being a leader means having the power to control others. Those who take this view eventually find that the more they try to control people, the less influence they have over them. For others, leadership means being in a position of authority. Yet a man can be a leader even if he's on the bottom of the totem pole. When a man sees that something must be done, he won't let his lack of position limit him from taking charge; he steps into the gap and assumes responsibility. True leadership is not about superiority, position or prestige. It's about revealing and releasing the potential of those around you. Leadership is not about the power of one, but facilitating the greatness of many.

Unfortunately many men today are sloughing off leadership responsibilities either because of laziness or apathy. They would rather live a life of ignoble ease and have others shoulder the responsibility for them. But the world needs the leadership of virtuous men more than ever. When you're called to serve as a leader, will you be ready to take on the challenge?

◄ FIVE TRAITS OF LEADERSHIP ►

"In any moment of decision, the best thing you can do is the right thing, the next best thing is the wrong thing, and the worst thing you can do is nothing."

—THEODORE ROOSEVELT

In 1950, the Department of Defense printed a small book, *The Armed Forces Officer*, which gave advice on how to become better leaders and men. In it, the authors listed five traits that make an effective leader. We've taken these traits and explored their meaning and application for every man, whether an officer or a civilian.

1. QUIET RESOLUTION

An effective leader has the resolve to see every task through to the end. Resolve is easy to have in the quiet before the storm comes. It is when the fear, chaos, and stress of a crisis hits that true resolve is revealed. At that moment, the man with quiet resolve does not waffle or STAND SHILLY-SHALLY. Without the terrible grip of indecision seizing him, he is cool and levelheaded, unflappable in the face of challenge. He is not loud, yelling and scurrying about in an attempt to cover his lack of grit with useless action. The man with quiet resolution is a man others can feel supremely confident in. While the world around him goes to pot, he knows what his mission is and he calmly fulfills it.

How to become a leader with quiet resolution: Do not wait for a crisis to emerge to make a decision. Inventory your values and goals, and set a plan for how you will react when certain crises arise and important decisions need to be made. Do not wait to make your choice until the heat of the moment, when you will be most tempted to surrender your values. Set a course for yourself, and when trials come and you are sorely tested, you will not panic, you will not waver, you will simply remember your plan and follow it through.

2. THE HARDIHOOD TO TAKE RISKS

Great achievements come to those who are willing to take risks. A leader who continually plays it safe will never put themselves or the people they lead in a position to experience success. A life without risks is surely alluring; its sweet lullaby of safety and comfort has lulled many a man into the trap of mediocrity and apathy. But a man who never dares greatly fails to see that he has taken the greatest risk of all: the risk that he will never progress, never refine his soul, never amount to anything worthwhile.

How to become a leader that takes risks: The fear of taking risks can be very real. You cannot expect to have the courage to take a large risk when you have had no experience taking small ones. So find opportunities in your daily life to take little risks. As you venture more risks, you develop the capacity to overcome your fear and gain the wisdom to know when a risk is worth taking. In this way, you will achieve the mettle to take the big risk when your leadership abilities are truly called upon.

3. THE READINESS TO SHARE IN REWARDS WITH SUBORDINATES

A great leader, although supremely confident, humbly acknowledges that no success, no matter how large of a role he personally played in bringing it to fruition, is wholly a solo effort. He is deeply grateful for everyone who played a part in the achievement, even those who had small roles. He understands that people love to be recognized for their contributions. When a person sees that a leader is humble and will share in success, they're more willing to follow that man.

How to become a leader who shares rewards with subordinates: Sharing success with the people who follow you can be as easy as offering public recognition or increasing their compensation. A simple thank-you card expressing your gratitude for an employee's effort in completing a project can go a long way. When offering thanks or giving praise, be as specific as possible. This shows the person you lead that you are keenly aware of what they do and makes the thanks or praise more personal and sincere.

4. AN EQUAL READINESS TO TAKE THE BLAME WHEN THINGS GO ADVERSELY

It is when things go wrong that true leaders are separated from the pretenders. An INFERNAL SKUNK of a leader will gladly accept the accolades when he and his team succeeds, but will find another individual to take the fall when things get tough. When followers see this, it completely demolishes their confidence and allegiance to that leader. True leaders, even when a subordinate is at fault, will take full responsibility for a mistake. An effective leader will then immediately take action to correct the situation.

How to be a leader by taking the blame when things go adversely: When shouldering the blame, you must do so sincerely. To accept blame, but to do so grudgingly, makes you a boy not a man. Never play the part of the martyr and seek glory for taking the fall. Likewise don't take the blame publicly, but then tell your subordinates that the only reason you took responsibility was to save their butts. You'll look like a phony and deteriorate their trust in you.

5. THE NERVE TO SURVIVE STORM AND DISAPPOINTMENT...

... and to face each new day with the score sheet wiped clean; neither dwelling on one's successes, nor accepting discouragement from one's failures. All of history's great leaders had moments of glorious success and moments of devastating defeat. Great leaders focus on the things they can change and influence, and the past is not one of those things. If you fail, learn from it but cease to dwell on it. When you succeed, celebrate with your followers and move on. A leader who continually dwells on past success shows that he has not set his eye on greater things. Additionally, as we learn from the Greeks, a leader's hubris can quickly become their downfall. Always stay humble and hungry.

How to become a leader by not living in the past: Read biographies of great leaders in history. By reading about the lives of these great men, you'll learn that even the best leaders faced enormous setbacks. You'll gain perspective and come to see that one failure does not mean the death of a man's capacity to lead. And the amazing feats of the great men of history will inspire you to believe in the powerful influence on history a true leader can wield.

Almost every leader exudes a certain amount of charisma. It's that intangible quality that magnetically pulls people toward him and makes them willing to buy what he's selling and follow him to the ends of the earth. While it is true that certain people are born with natural charisma, it's possible for those who weren't so genetically blessed to develop this winning attribute.

Disarm to charm. The key to charisma can be found in this nifty motto. When a man's warmth, attentiveness and intrigue confound a person's expectations, they will let down their guard and thus be open to your suggestions and powers of persuasion.

Act intently interested. The truest mark of a charismatic man is his ability to make another feel as though they are the most important person in the room. He locks into a conversation and creates a cocoon around the other person and himself. He seems unbothered by any distractions and acts genuinely interested in what the other person has to say. How do you do this? **(FIGURE 7.1)**

- Keep steady eye contact with the person. Don't bore your eyeballs into theirs as if you are about to project laser beams from your retinas. To achieve the right amount of intensity, look into their eyes while occasionally flitting yours to the sides of their head.

- Signal that you are listening. Nod your IDEA-POT from time to time. Throw in noises and words like "uh-huh," "I see," "hmmmm," "right," etc.

- Make sure the other person does the most talking. Ask them questions about what they are most interested in. Then, as they tell you stories, ask follow-up questions and request that they explain their statements further.

FIGURE 7.1 The truest mark of a charismatic man is his ability to make another feel as though they are the most important person in the room.

- Use the person's name. Everyone loves the sound of their own name. Using another's name during conversation makes you seem warm and personable. It also shows that you were paying attention during introductions and that the other person was important enough for you to memorize their name. However, avoid overusing a person's name. Too much name use will make you sound like a sketchy car salesman.

Cultivate a little mystery. Charisma is like a fire that needs space and oxygen to survive. If you are a completely open book, you'll smother the flame. People follow a charismatic leader because they create an aura around themselves that allow others to believe they are in some way different; they have insights into the world inaccessible to the average Joe. If everyone knows you drive a Honda Civic, play fantasy football, eat Taco Bell three times a week and have never left the country, they're not going to believe you have special and mysterious powers. A little mysterious aloofness will leave others intrigued and desiring to unlock your secrets.

Employ mimicry. Imitation is the sincerest form of flattery, and one of the best methods of building charisma. Studies have proven that by carefully and subtly imitating another person's body language and speaking style, you build instant social rapport, goodwill and trust. When speaking with another person, watch and then mirror their body position and speech patterns; if they cross their legs, you cross your legs; if they lean back, you lean back; if they speak slowly, you speak slowly. Always wait about two to three seconds before mirroring someone's behavior. And make your mimicry subtle and inexact. If you copy someone perfectly, your mimicry will be too obvious, the person will catch on and your plan will backfire in a big way. Nobody likes to be mocked.

Smile. Few things have the power to disarm like a warm and genuine smile. It lures people in like a tractor beam.

Be generous in your compliments. Nobody feels good about themselves all the time; everybody's been the fat kid picked last for kick ball once in his life and as a result is walking around a bit wounded. The charming man is always looking for opportunities to boost the self-esteem of others. Compliment others on things both big and small.

Use self-deprecating humor. Even the charming man occasionally gets into trouble; but no matter how big the pile of poo he's fallen in, he knows the secret of coming out smelling like a rose. Some men think a leader should never admit mistakes; quite to the contrary, the charismatic leader fesses up to blunders–but he does so with a smile and a bit of humor. By not taking yourself too seriously, you become more approachable and attractive to others.

HOW TO SHAKE HANDS LIKE A MAN

On your path to great success and glory, you're going to meet hundreds of people who can either help you move up in the world or hinder your progress. It is therefore essential that you cultivate the ability to make a dynamite first impression. In addition to dressing well and exuding charisma, the ability to perform a manly handshake is an essential component in your first-impression arsenal. Make no mistake about it: A handshake says a lot about a man. Will your new contact think you've recently been scaling Mount Olympus or will he write you off as a Wimpy McWimpsalot? **(FIGURE 7.2)**

How You Do It

Many an introduction has been instantly marred by man extending a dead fish instead of a hearty hand. So save the albacore for dinner and make sure the grip of your handshake is firm and confident. However, you don't want to crush the other person's hand.

- Aim for a full grip, not a finger shake. Make sure the web in between your thumb and index finger connects with their web.

FIGURE 7.2 In addition to dressing well and exuding charisma, the ability to perform a manly handshake is an essential component in your first-impression arsenal.

- Make sure you don't have food or grease on your hands. You want the person to remember you, not your penchant for Cheetos.
- If your hands are sweaty, give them a quick nonchalant wipe on your DRUMSTICK CASES. Holding your hand open previous to the shake instead of clenching it will help prevent sweatiness.
- When you offer your hand, look the person in the eye and smile.
- When shaking a woman's hand, allow her to be the one to offer it. If she does, give her a firm handshake. Women do not appreciate a HANDSHAKE LIKE A WILTED PETUNIA.
- No joy buzzers. Unless you're meeting the dean of clown school.

WHEN YOU DO IT

Handshakes involve effective timing. Many people avoid offering handshakes because they're afraid they might be left hanging. If you're not sure if someone will notice your offer, extend the handshake anyway. Most of the time people will notice your outstretched hand and quickly grasp it.

Be aware that in some cultures the handshake is not an appropriate greeting. In countries like Thailand and India, for example, you will be expected to press your hands together and bow. Be sensitive to these types of cultural differences.

MANLY ADVICE

WHAT IF YOU'RE LEFT HANGING?

It's hard not to feel dumb when your hand is left flapping in the breeze, especially when everyone but the person with whom you were trying to shake hands saw the rejection. Don't feel embarrassed. The problem isn't that the other person doesn't think you're important, your timing was just off. To avoid this scenario:

- Don't offer a handshake if the other person is engrossed in conversation with someone else.
- Don't approach someone from the side with your extended hand. It's hard to see.
- Do audibly greet the person first to get their attention and then offer your hand.
- If you are left hanging, while it's tempting, don't take your unshaken hand, run it through your hair, and say, "Go bake a cake," in order to save face.

◄ PREPARE AND DELIVER A DYNAMITE SPEECH ►

"You have enemies? Good. That means you've stood up for something, sometime in your life."

—WINSTON CHURCHILL

The power of the spoken word is undeniable. Great speeches have motivated citizens to fight injustice, drawn meaning out of tragedy and memorialized events with the dignity and solemnity they deserved. Words can change the course of history or alter the path of an individual's life.

While most men will never summon troops into battle or debate a congressional bill, every man should strive to be a great orator. Whether it is giving the best man speech, arguing against a policy at a city council, making a proposal at work or giving a eulogy, you will be asked to publicly speak at least a few times in your life. Don't be a man that shakes and shudders at that thought. Be a man who welcomes, nay, relishes the opportunity to move and inspire people with the power of his words. When a speaking opportunity arises, be the guy everyone thinks of first. When duty calls, here's how to rise to the occasion.

PREPARE YOUR SPEECH

1. Establish the purpose of the speech. Before you start writing, determine what the purpose of you speech will be. Is to inform? To entertain? To persuade? To motivate? To convince your friends of the benefits of male garters? When you figure out your purpose, write it down. This will help keep your research and organization focused.

2. Research. First, look into your audience's background. What motivates them? What are their concerns? By knowing these things, you'll be able to craft a speech specifically designed for your listeners. You can easily find out about your audience by asking the person who assigned you the topic for some background information.

Next, you'll want to research your topic. This is a good idea even if you're an expert in your field. Perhaps you can find something new about your topic or a fresh angle that would be particularly interesting to your audience.

2. Outline. The best way to start outlining is to list all the points you would like to make in your speech. Go crazy. When you're done, go through your list and pick the three most important points that will help you achieve your original purpose.

After you have your three important points, organize them in a logical order in an outline. You can organize it chronologically or present the problems with their respective solutions.

3. Write out your speech. Even if you don't plan on reading from it or even using notes, it's always a good idea to write the speech out. It will help focus your thoughts, give you something to study and prevent you from rambling like a crazy person at the podium. Having a well-written speech in hand and knowing exactly what you plan to say will also give you a boost of confidence.

4. Start off with a killer opening. Most people usually start off with a joke of some sort, hoping to break the ice. This is a big risk, because if the joke falls flat, you've pretty much killed any possible rapport with the audience.

Another great way to start a speech is to immediately relate the topic back to the audience. From the get-go your listeners will be engaged because they know that the speech affects them. You also can't go wrong with starting the speech with a story. A good story at the beginning of a speech will pique the interest of your listeners and emotionally engage them.

No matter what approach you take, make sure to actually reveal the topic to your audience in the introduction. You don't want to leave them in dark about your subject until the end of the speech.

5. Use personal anecdotes. You want to connect with your audience when you're speaking. The best way to connect with any person is to share something personal about yourself. Your life is full of experiences and stories to which the members of your audience can relate.

6. Talk like a normal person. When writing your speech, don't use JAW TWISTERS that sound "smart." You probably don't talk like that in your daily life, so don't do it in your speeches.

7. End with a bang. The easiest way to end a speech is to summarize the main points. This ensures that your audience walks away knowing exactly what you wished to convey to them. If the purpose of your speech is to arouse people to action, conclude with a call to action. Use language that stirs the audience's passions and structure your sentences to crescendo to an emotional climax. No matter how you end your speech, make sure it's brief, or you'll dilute its impact.

DELIVER YOUR SPEECH

1. Practice. Practice. Practice. Before you deliver your actual speech, you should have practiced it at least a dozen times. You can also practice where to put oratorical flares like pauses, hand gestures and voice inflections. Practice in front of a mirror. Practice in front of a friend and ask for honest feedback.

2. Look sharp. Don't show up looking like the only speeches you've given have been to the birds in the park. Let your dress reflect the content and tone of the speech. For a more formal or persuasive speech, wear a suit or at least a sport coat and slacks. If the speech is about your adventures in Africa, don your safari vest. Regardless, always look sharp. The audience will respect you and you'll feel more self-assured.

3. Stand up straight. Again, you want to project supreme confidence. No one wants to listen to Quasimodo talk to his shoes.

4. Vary your tone. Nothing will put your audience to sleep faster than a visit from android man from the year 2050. Short-circuit the monotonous robot voice and keep things interesting by adding vocal inflections as you speak. Use inflections to reveal that you're asking a question, being sarcastic or conveying excitement. You already do this naturally in everyday conversation.

5. Master the pause. Most people are so nervous when they get up to speak that they rush through the whole thing like the Micro Machines guy. But they're losing out on employing one of the most powerful oratory techniques—the pause. A pause can add a bit of dramatic flair to a statement or it can help the audience really drink up an idea. The key with a pause is timing. Use it only at spots where it will be effective. "Hello (pause) my (pause) name is (pause)," would not be such a time. Practice inserting pauses in your speech to find what works.

6. Look your audience in the eye. When you look people in the eye, you make a connection. But how can you look an entire audience in the eye? As you go through your speech, work your way across the room making eye contact with each person in the audience. Maintain eye

FIGURE 7.3 If used effectively, hand gestures can give added emphasis to your words. Don't worry too much about hand gestures; just let them flow naturally.

contact for a few seconds. If it's too short, you'll seem nervous and shifty. If you look too long, you'll start creeping people out.

7. Let gestures flow naturally. If used effectively, hand gestures can give added emphasis to your words. If used incorrectly, you'll end up looking like an octopus having a seizure. Don't worry too much about hand gestures; just let them flow naturally. You might want to have someone watch you deliver your speech before the big day to make sure your natural gesticulation isn't distracting. If it is, adjust accordingly, but don't obsess about it. Especially if you're Italian; thatsa your heritage! **(FIGURE 7.3)**

OVERCOMING THE FEAR OF PUBLIC SPEAKING

Speaking in public is one of the most common phobias because people are afraid of looking stupid and embarrassing themselves in front of a large audience. Here are two things you can do to help overcome your fear of public speaking.

Take advantage of any opportunity to speak in front of people. The best way to conquer a fear is to confront it head-on. Find any opportunities available to speak in front of others, even if that means giving the announcements at an office meeting or reading aloud a passage in class. These small steps will help get you ready to stand at the orator's podium.

Realize your audience doesn't usually notice your mistakes. Even if they do catch a slipup, they probably won't care. Audiences are a sympathetic bunch. They understand how nerve-racking it can be to speak in public. Just keep speaking until tomatoes are thrown or you feel a cane around your neck.

MANLY ADVICE

TEN GREAT
SPEECHES TO STUDY

If a man wishes to become a great orator, he must first become a student of the great orators who have come before him. He must immerse himself in their speeches, reading and listening for the turns of phrases and textual symmetries, the pauses and crescendos, the metaphors and melodies that have enabled the greatest speeches to stand the test of time. Here are ten speeches every man should familiarize himself with.

1. Winston Churchill, "We Shall Fight on the Beaches," June 4, 1940
2. Demosthenes, "The Third Philippic," 342 B.C.
3. John F. Kennedy, "Inauguration Address," January 20, 1961

4. Pericles, "Funeral Oration," 431 B.C.
5. Frederick Douglass, "What to the Slave is the Fourth of July?" July 5, 1852
6. General Douglas MacArthur, "Duty, Honor, Country," May 12, 1962
7. Theodore Roosevelt, "Citizenship in a Republic," April 23, 1910
8. Franklin Delano Roosevelt, "Pearl Harbor Address to the Nation," December 8, 1941
9. Martin Luther King Jr., "I Have a Dream," August 28, 1963
10. Abraham Lincoln, "The Gettysburg Address," November 19, 1863

GIVE AND ACCEPT CRITICISM ◀ WITHOUT COMING OFF LIKE A CAD ▶

"Nearly all men can stand adversity, but if you want to test a man's character, give him power."

—ABRAHAM LINCOLN

It's not the most pleasant part of the job, but every leader must be adept at both taking and receiving criticism. Receiving criticism helps us improve, for it is other people who can point out the mistakes and shortcomings that we can't see ourselves. And dispensing constructive criticism increases your team or organization's chances for success. Unfortunately many young men today don't know how to offer and accept criticism like a man. Instead they handle criticism like little boys. When giving criticism, they opt only to give snide, cutting jabs that do nothing to improve the situation. When receiving criticism, they sulk, make excuses and argue with the person criticizing them.

Because we all face situations every day that require us to give or take criticism, we provide the following guidelines on how to make the process more constructive.

How to Give Effective Criticism

Go in cool, calm and collected. Before you begin to give criticism, make sure you have your emotions in check. This is particularly important if the person did something that really ticked you off. If you go in yelling and banging your fist on desks, you'll probably get the problem fixed in the short term. However, you miss out on an opportunity to solve the underlying issues.

Start with the positives. Before criticizing someone, it's always good to point out the things that they've been doing well. Then transition into your criticism by saying something like, "There is just one area I thought could use improvement..." Two benefits exist from this exercise. First, it will make the criticism easier to swallow by reminding the person they're not a complete screw-up. Second, it shows the person what they're doing right and gives them a reference point on which to base future work. **(FIGURE 7.4)**

Be specific. If there's one thing you remember, let it be this: Be as specific as you can in your critiques. Don't just tell the person, "This sucks," or "This could be better." Explain exactly why their work or action is subpar. A blanket criticism will put the person on the defensive, and they'll never be able to correct their problem.

Criticize the action, not the person. Avoid making your criticism personal, and focus only on the person's actions instead. This makes the criticism less hurtful and much more effective. So don't say things like, "Jeez Louise you must be an idiot! Look at all these mistakes you

FIGURE 7.4 Before criticizing someone, it's always good to point out the things that they've been doing well. Then transition into your criticism.

made in this report!" Just because someone makes a mistake doesn't mean that person is a pinhead. We all have bad days.

Be a diplomat. When giving your specific criticism, it sometimes helps to use diplomatic words. Our old friend Benjamin Franklin was a master at this (which is why he was probably such a successful diplomat). In his autobiography, Franklin said this about using diplomatic language in discussion:

"When I advance anything that may possibly be disputed, [I never use] the words certainly, undoubtedly, or any others that give the air of positiveness to an opinion; but rather say, I conceive or apprehend a thing to be so and so; it appears to me, or I should think it so or so, for such and such reasons; or I imagine it to be so; or it is so, if I am not mistaken."

Using such diplomatic words removes the sharp edge from your criticism. Sometimes, however, people need that edge to spur them to action. Use your discretion in deciding whether a harsher approach would be more appropriate.

Make specific suggestions for improvement. The goal of criticism should be to help someone make improvements. While specifically pointing out the problem is the first step to correction, if a person doesn't know what they can do to improve, knowing their mistakes won't help them one bit. Don't just tell people what's wrong with their work, give them specific suggestions on how they can improve it. The key word, once again, is *specific*.

Follow up. Always, always follow up after giving constructive criticism. Your criticism won't do any good if the person doesn't put your suggestions into practice. Schedule a follow-up with the person you've critiqued. Say something like, "How about we meet together next week to see how your changes are coming and to answer any new questions you might have?" By letting the person know you'll be following up with them, they're more likely to get their butt in gear and make the needed corrections.

HOW TO TAKE CRITICISM

Consider the source. You're going to receive criticism from thousands of people in your lifetime. It's important to remember that not all criticism is created equal. If you think the source of your criticism isn't genuinely interested in helping you improve, take their criticism with a grain of salt. At the same time, be sure to honestly assess your critic's point. Some people are too quick to write off criticism by saying, "They're just jealous!" Maybe so, but be sure to thoughtfully evaluate the feedback before dismissing it.

Shut your trap and listen. Fight the urge to argue with the person or explain your mistake, and just open your ears. You'd be surprised what you can learn if you simply soak it in.

Don't take it personally. Try to detach yourself as much as possible from your actions or work when receiving criticism so you can look at it objectively. This can be hard to do, particularly if you put a lot of time and effort into something. But trust me, if you make this a habit when receiving criticism, you'll save yourself from a bruised ego.

Stay calm (even if the other person is being a complete scalawag). If your critic is being a WELL-MEANING, PINHEADED, ANARCHISTIC CRANK, staying calm can be hard to do. But be the better man. Let the other person do all their ranting and raving, while you sit there looking cool as a cucumber. When they're done, kill them with kindness. Let them know you understand their concern and thank them for taking the time to bring it to your attention.

Ask clarifying questions. Clarifying questions are particularly important if your critic gives vague or ambiguous criticism. For example, if your critic tells you your report isn't clear, ask them where things start to get murky and suggestions on how it can be improved. By asking questions, you create dialogue between you and your critic, which in turns fosters cooperation and an atmosphere for mutual improvement.

Take ownership of your mistake. When someone brings a legitimate mistake to your attention, don't get on the defensive and start making excuses for it. Take responsibility for your actions. While denying your mistakes can keep the heat off for a moment, it will greatly impede your personal progress in the long run.

Change your perspective on criticism. Instead of seeing criticism as humiliating or embarrassing, view it as an opportunity to improve yourself. Winston Churchill had this to say about criticism:

"Criticism may not be agreeable, but it is necessary. It fulfills the same function as pain in the human body. It calls attention to an unhealthy state of things."

Instead of avoiding criticism, seek for opportunities to be criticized. You'll find that getting feedback from an outside source will stretch your talents and abilities.

Thank your critic (even when he handed your butt to you). This can be difficult. No one seriously wants to say, "Thanks for showing me that I was wrong!" But swallow your pride and sincerely thank your critic. They took the time to sit down with you and point out areas where you can improve. The least you can do is say thanks.

Take action and follow up. After you've received your criticism, take action immediately. After you've taken action, make sure to follow up with your critic and let them know how you've rectified the problem. This shows that you actually listened to the criticism and respected what the person had to say.

"IF"
BY RUDYARD KIPLING

Many leaders have seen the wisdom in memorizing poems and passages from great books, filling their minds with inspiring words to have at the ready whenever their soul is troubled. If there is one poem you should consider committing to memory, let it be Rudyard Kipling's "If." (To help you memorize this classic poem, there is a card in the back of this book that you can cut out and carry in your wallet.) There is perhaps no better metric in the written canon on one's leadership and manhood.

> If you can keep your head when all about you
> Are losing theirs and blaming it on you,
> If you can trust yourself when all men doubt you
> But make allowance for their doubting too,
> If you can wait and not be tired by waiting,
> Or being lied about, don't deal in lies,

Or being hated, don't give way to hating,
And yet don't look too good, nor talk too wise:

If you can dream—and not make dreams your master,
If you can think—and not make thoughts your aim;
If you can meet with Triumph and Disaster
And treat those two impostors just the same;
If you can bear to hear the truth you've spoken
Twisted by knaves to make a trap for fools,
Or watch the things you gave your life to, broken,
And stoop and build 'em up with worn-out tools:
If you can make one heap of all your winnings
And risk it all on one turn of pitch-and-toss,
And lose, and start again at your beginnings
And never breathe a word about your loss;
If you can force your heart and nerve and sinew
To serve your turn long after they are gone,
And so hold on when there is nothing in you
Except the Will which says to them: "Hold on!"

If you can talk with crowds and keep your virtue,
Or walk with kings—nor lose the common touch,
If neither foes nor loving friends can hurt you;
If all men count with you, but none too much,
If you can fill the unforgiving minute
With sixty seconds' worth of distance run,
Yours is the Earth and everything that's in it,
And—which is more—you'll be a Man, my son!

CHAPTER EIGHT

THE VIRTUOUS MAN

"In the great battle of life, no brilliancy of intellect, no perfection of bodily development, will count when weighed in the balance against the assemblage of virtues, active and passive, of moral qualities which we group together under the name of character."

—THEODORE ROOSEVELT

Virtue has gotten a bad rap in the modern age. It is often seen solely as a religious preoccupation or unfairly saddled with sissy or effeminate associations. However, virtue is far from being the domain of the pansy. Actually the word *virtue* is firmly rooted in manliness. *Virtue* comes from the Latin virtus, which in turn is derived from *vir*, Latin for *manliness*. Thus, when ancient philosophers like Aristotle encouraged men to live "the virtuous life," they were essentially calling for men to man up.

One man took on Aristotle's challenge to live the virtuous, or manly, life with particular fervor: Benjamin Franklin. Franklin's pursuit was not a religious one and can be embraced by any man, no matter his particular set of beliefs. Franklin's quest should be the mission of every man: to become the best man he can possibly be and thus be of greatest service to his country, community and family.

FRANKLIN'S QUEST FOR MORAL PERFECTION

Benjamin Franklin, the original self-made man, is an American legend. Despite being born into a poor family and receiving only two years of formal schooling, Franklin became a successful printer, scientist, musician and author. Oh, and in his spare time he helped found a country and then served as its diplomat.

The key to Franklin's success was his drive to constantly improve himself. In 1726, at the age of twenty, Ben Franklin set his loftiest goal: the attainment of moral perfection.

"I conceiv'd the bold and arduous project of arriving at moral perfection. I wish'd to live without committing any fault at any time; I would conquer all that either natural inclination, custom, or company might lead me into."

In order to accomplish his goal, Franklin developed and committed himself to a personal improvement program that consisted of living thirteen virtues. The thirteen virtues were:

"TEMPERANCE. Eat not to dullness; drink not to elevation."

"SILENCE. Speak not but what may benefit others or yourself; avoid trifling conversation."

"ORDER. Let all your things have their places; let each part of your business have its time."

"RESOLUTION. Resolve to perform what you ought; perform without fail what you resolve."

"FRUGALITY. Make no expense but to do good to others or yourself; i.e., waste nothing."

"INDUSTRY. Lose no time; be always employ'd in something useful; cut off all unnecessary actions."

"SINCERITY. Use no hurtful deceit; think innocently and justly, and, if you speak, speak accordingly."

"JUSTICE. Wrong none by doing injuries, or omitting the benefits that are your duty."

"MODERATION. Avoid extremes; forbear resenting injuries so much as you think they deserve."

"CLEANLINESS. Tolerate no uncleanliness in body, clothes, or habitation."

"TRANQUILLITY. Be not disturbed at trifles, or at accidents common or unavoidable."

"CHASTITY. Rarely use venery but for health or offspring, never to dullness, weakness, or the injury of your own or another's peace or reputation."

"HUMILITY. Imitate Jesus and Socrates."

In order to keep track of his adherence to these virtues, Franklin carried a small book of thirteen charts. The charts consisted of a column for each day of the week and thirteen rows marked with the first letter of his thirteen virtues. At the end of each day Franklin placed a dot next to each virtue he violated. The goal was to minimize the number of marks, thus indicating a "clean" life, free of vice.

Franklin focused on one particular virtue each week by placing it at the top of that week's chart and including a short precept explaining its meaning. After he had moved through all thirteen virtues, he'd start the process over again.

INDUSTRY

Lose no time.
Be always employed in something useful.
Cut off all unnecessary actions.

	SU	M	TU	W	TH	F	SA
TE							
SIL							
O							
R							
F							
I							
SIN							
J							
M							
CL							
TR							
CH							
H							

When Franklin first started his program, he found himself putting marks in the book more than he desired. But as time went by, he saw the marks diminish.

While Franklin never accomplished his goal of moral perfection (his passion for beer, food and women are well documented), he found that simply making the attempt was reward enough.

"Tho' I never arrived at the perfection I had been so ambitious of obtaining, but fell far short of it, yet I was, by the endeavour, a better and a happier man than I otherwise should have been if I had not attempted it."

APPLYING FRANKLIN'S PURSUIT OF "THE VIRTUOUS LIFE" TO YOUR LIFE

"A man does what he must—in spite of personal consequences, in spite of obstacles and dangers and pressures—and that is the basis of all human morality."

—WINSTON CHURCHILL

It's time for men to reclaim the association between manliness and virtue. Start manning up and follow Franklin's example of striving to improve yourself each and every day. Of course, Franklin lived in a different time and place than today's men. Therefore, to help you on the course of self-improvement, we have explored how each of Franklin's virtues can be applied to the life of a modern man.

Begin the process by cutting out Franklin's virtue chart in the back of this book. Carry the chart around just as Franklin did, as a constant reminder of your quest to live a virtuous life. See if you can go a whole day without having to give yourself a mark for not living the virtues.

TEMPERANCE

"Eat not to dullness; drink not to elevation."

Is there a less sexy idea today than temperance? Yet when Benjamin Franklin began his pursuit of the virtuous life, he chose to concentrate on this virtue first. The way in which Ben ordered his thirteen virtues was deliberate. He selected temperance to kick off his self-improvement program in the belief that first attaining self-discipline in the area of food and drink would make adherence to all of the other virtues easier.

Why is this? Hunger and thirst are some of the most primal of urges and therefore are some of the hardest to control. Thus, when seeking to gain self-discipline a man must start with his most basic appetites and work up from there. A man must first harness his inward urges before tackling the more external virtues. A clear mind and a healthy body are prerequisites to the pursuit of the virtuous life.

Eat Not to Dullness

Have you ever noticed that the first few bites of a delicious food are the best? But after chowing down on something for awhile, the vibrant tastes become significantly dulled.

Today many men shovel food into their mouths so fast that their palate never has a chance to register this transition. Yet the shift is one of the ways the stomach tries to tell the brain that it's full and to stop eating. Unfortunately men ignore this signal and continue eating far past it. The consequence is not only a far less enjoyable eating experience but an ever-expanding gut.

There are a million diet books and health magazines out there, but the only thing a man needs to know to maintain a decent waistline is this: Eat when hungry, stop when full. Don't eat in front of the TV or on the go. Sit down for a proper meal. Savor each mouthful, and think about the flavors you are experiencing. Put your fork down between bites. When the flavors become less vibrant and your stomach starts to feel full, stop eating. **(FIGURE 8.1)**

Drink Not to Elevation

Many a manly man in history has enjoyed a drink or two. Yet somewhere along the way, it became acceptable for men to imbibe their spirits through a funnel and throw back shot after shot of Jägermeister. But there's nothing manly about being a GUZZLE GUTS.

At the heart of manliness is the belief in personal responsibility. But excess drinking and personal responsibility are at odds. When drunk, men are not 100 percent in control of their choices. So if something goes wrong, they often blame the alcohol. A true man is fully present and completely in control of himself in every situation.

Men should also seek to rid themselves of any kind of dependencies. Alcohol can cause several, the most obvious one being outright alcoholism. But frequent boozing can also make a man dependent on

FIGURE 8.1 Sit down for a proper meal. Savor each mouthful, and think about the flavors you are experiencing.

liquor for confidence and a good time. It becomes a crutch. True men are confident and dynamic enough on their own. They don't need liquid courage to create their fun or to be more charming.

SILENCE

"Speak not but what may benefit others or yourself; avoid trifling conversation."

Ben was not referring to monastic solitude when he presented silence as a virtue. Instead he had in mind the ability of knowing the appropriate time and words to speak. In our world full of talking heads, it seems if you want to grab attention and respect, you must speak over other people. But while these blowhards may get our attention, they hardly earn our respect.

Calvin "Silent Cal" Coolidge had this virtue down to a science. Turning to the president at dinner, author and poet Dorothy Parker, said, "Mr. Coolidge, I've made a bet against a fellow who said it was impossible to get more than two words out of you." Coolidge's reply? "You lose."

THE BENEFITS
OF PRACTICING SILENCE

You can observe more. The guy who sits back quietly while others are yammering away is often the one with the keenest insights in a debate. And he frequently knows more about his group of friends than anyone else.

You add a commanding mystique to your character. The man who remains silent and only speaks when he has something important to say engenders great respect. When this man opens his mouth, others shut theirs. They know that this man speaks only when it's edifying, so what he has to say must be important.

It allows you to distinguish yourself with your actions. Nothing is manlier than a man who rolls up his sleeves and gets to work without uttering so much as a word. While many men spend their time filling the air with talk of lofty aspirations, the man who succeeds in life spends his time actually getting things done.

Practicing the Virtue of Silence

Listen more than you speak. We could all benefit a great deal if we opened our ears and shut our mouth more often. Make it a goal in each conversation to speak less than the other person.

Think before you open your mouth. Many a man has had to stick his foot in his mouth from time to time. These embarrassing slips of the tongue can easily be prevented if a man takes some time to think about what he's about to say.

Don't fear the silence. As you interact with others, lulls in conversation will inevitably arise. When conversing with new acquaintances, filling in these gaps is considered polite and sociable. But once you become more intimate with someone, the nervous need to constantly fill the silence will come off as insecure. A comfortable silence builds rapport just as well as ceaseless chatter.

Fill your mind with virtuous and well-ordered thoughts. When people apologize for lacking a brain to mouth filter, their real problem is not a porous sieve but a disorderly mind. What you speak is a mirror of what you think. Filling your mind with positive, clear, intelligent thoughts will ensure that what you speak will benefit others and yourself.

ORDER

"Let all your things have their places; let each part of your business have its time."

Franklin chose order as his third virtue because it "would allow [him] more time for attending to [his] projects and [his] studies." Franklin understood that if he wanted to get important things done in his life, he had to make sure the little things wouldn't get in the way.

The lives of men today are far busier and distraction filled than Ben could ever have imagined. Unfortunately today's society too often equates unfettered masculinity with chaos and sloppiness. Yet this association is patently false; just ask your local drill sergeant.

In the military, a great amount of time and energy is spent on instilling the virtue of order. When a recruit enters basic training, he quickly learns to perfectly make his bed, neatly pack his possessions in his footlocker and religiously shine his shoes. He learns to eat, shower and dress far more efficiently than he ever thought possible. If a soldier does not meet these standards, he is swiftly punished. So what's the big deal? What does the military understand about order that many civilian men overlook?

Order develops attention to detail. In the armed forces, details can mean the difference between life and death. Even a mundane task like keeping an orderly bunk strengthens a soldier's eye for detail. Attention to detail is important in civilian life as well. The man who has an eye for details is more likely to succeed in his career than the man who doesn't.

Order creates standardization. Each armed force has a standard way it wants its soldiers to organize their bunk. By maintaining orderly surroundings, soldiers can focus on what's truly important. When a soldier is awakened in the middle of the night because his unit is under attack, the last thing he wants to think about is where he put his gun. Likewise, creating standardization in your own life helps you focus on your highest priorities.

Creating Order in Your Life

Create systems. Creating orderly systems allows you to free up valuable mental resources to devote to more important matters. For example, establishing a place in your home to put your keys, wallet and cell phone will enable you to pick them up each day without having to frantically search for them.

Another system you can set up is batching. Batching is grouping similar activities together and doing them all at once. For example, instead of wasting time throughout the day checking and answering e-mails, check and answer them all at once.

Automate. Look for areas in your life that can be put on autopilot. One area in your life that you can easily implement this is your personal finances. Most banks provide automatic bill-paying services and depositing. Set it up, forget about it and get to work on conquering the world.

Plan weekly. Every Sunday set aside an hour to plan your coming week. Formulating an attack plan will keep you focused on your priorities.

Do it now! The greatest single way to increase order in your life is to adopt "Do it now!" as your daily mantra. After you get out of bed, turn around and make it. After you receive a piece of mail, take action on it immediately. If you drop a sock on the floor, pick it up without hesitation. It's not as easy as it sounds; the natural tendency of the entire universe is to go from order to chaos. Overcome this pull to the path of least resistance by repeating the mantra "Do it now!" and pushing through this force. By employing the "do it now" rule, things will never pile up to the point that setting them right seems like an insurmountable task.

RESOLUTION

"Resolve to perform what you ought; perform without fail what you resolve."

In 1912, while campaigning for a third term as president in Milwaukee, Wisconsin, Theodore Roosevelt was shot in the chest at close range by a would-be assassin. The bullet, slowed by a steel eyeglasses case and a folded speech, lodged in his rib.

Roosevelt's manly resolve was unwavering. Refusing medical attention, he insisted on proceeding to the auditorium where ten thousand people waited to hear his speech. Mounting the stage he showed the audience his bloody shirt and said:

"I have just been shot, but it takes more than that to kill a bull moose."

TR then spoke for a full ninety minutes before finally consenting to be taken to a hospital.

Resolution is a virtue that is as needed in crisis situations like the one Roosevelt faced as it is with daily mundane tasks. Franklin included resolution as his fourth virtue, because attaining it would ensure he would work through the other nine. He understood that resolution is the virtue that all other successes in life are predicated on.

The virtue of resolution is one that marks a man's passage from boy to man. A boy will dabble in a thousand pursuits and then drop them when he gets bored or they become too difficult. A man will always finish what he starts. The virtue of resolution is thus inextricably tied up with that of integrity. The resolute man does what he says he will do, no matter what the cost.

Developing Your Resolution

Resolve how you will act when faced with a challenge, before you are faced with it. Three presidents had been assassinated during Roosevelt's lifetime, and he had long prepared himself to meet a similar fate. Such forethought allowed him to remain levelheaded and resolute when it happened. Like TR, there are certain physical and ethical tests you will assuredly face during your life. Decide now how you will handle these challenges, and when you're put to the test, you won't be tempted to THROW UP THE SPONGE.

Make an educated decision. When deciding which course to pursue in life, take some time to study the options and gather as much information on them as possible. Once you have come to a decision, write down the reasons for your choice. This way, as you take on a project or a journey, and times get tough, you can return to your journal, remember why you made the decision in the first place, and feel confident in continuing to move forward.

Don't look back. Resolution requires the cultivation of single-minded determination. Continually looking back and asking "What if?" will severely impede your progress. It's tempting to straddle the fence and try to have it both ways. Yet in attempting to live in two choices at once, you will find that you truly inhabit neither one. Regret is the arch nemesis of resolution.

Write down your goals every day. It's easy to be distracted by the mundane details of life and have them cloud your vision of greater things. Cut through this haze by writing down your goals every day. This action will keep you focused on the task you wish to accomplish and motivated to maintain your resolve.

FRUGALITY

"Make no expense but to do good to others or yourself; i.e., waste nothing."

I was once watching a TV show in which a roundtable of gurus was dispensing financial advice to the studio audience. One of the advisors suggested people give up little luxuries like a daily Starbucks run and save and invest that money instead. A woman in the audience stood up and cried, "But what if I don't want to give up Starbucks?" The crowd roared and clapped in approval. And a member of the Greatest Generation rolled over in his grave.

How to Be Frugal

We could cover some of the thousands of personal finance tips found in numerous books and websites on the subject. But all that info obscures a very simple fact: Being frugal is insanely easy. Here's what you do: Don't spend more than you take in. If you can't afford something, don't buy it. That's it.

So if frugality is so simple, why don't more men embrace it? They simply don't see the benefits. Men today, suckled on the teat of MTV's *Cribs* and raised in a culture of entitlement, see frugality only in terms of sacrifice. Frugality is thus in need of some serious rebranding (hiring Ebenezer Scrooge as its spokesperson was a big mistake). Because frugality is not so much about buying toilet paper by the pallet as it is about manning up and embracing an independent, self-reliant and truly authentic life.

Why Being Frugal Is Essential to Manning Up

Frugality keeps you out of bondage. MANEUVERING THE APOSTLES may seem like an easy way to buy whatever you want, but eventually it will catch up with you. Debt is slavery. The interest that accompanies high consumer debt never sleeps or dies. If you can't pay it, it will crush you. Frugality frees you from these shackles and affords you the liberty of financial independence.

Frugality helps you be self-reliant. Your grandfather lived by the mantra: "Use it up, wear it out, make it do, or do without." Of course it's hard to "make it do" if you don't know how to fix it. So learn some invaluable handyman skills and start enjoying one of the manliest satisfactions in life: knowing you can skip the repairman's bill and do it yourself. **(FIGURE 8.2)**

Frugality creates an authentic self. Our consumerist society wants us to believe that we are what we buy. But despite what advertisers tell us, we are made up of the things that cannot be purchased—our values, ethics, minds, relationships and hobbies. Frugality forces you to find an identity that can't be bought off the shelf. Instead of buying an SUV or a North Face jacket to feel outdoorsy, you go camping. Instead of buying expensive free trade coffee, you serve at a soup kitchen. By making the decision not to spend your money on stuff to make you feel better, you can start spending time developing the habits and traits that will make you a better man.

FIGURE 8.2 Learn some invaluable handyman skills and start enjoying one of the manliest satisfactions in life: knowing you can skip the repairman's bill and do it yourself.

INDUSTRY

"Lose no time. Be always employed in something useful. Cut off all unnecessary actions."

What Benjamin Franklin called "industry," Theodore Roosevelt called living the "strenuous life." TR's dedication to sucking the marrow out of life is unparalleled. His hard work and enthusiasm allowed him to do all of the following things during his sixty years of life:

- Work as state legislator, police commissioner and governor in New York
- Own and work a ranch in the Dakotas
- Serve as Assistant Secretary of the Navy
- Organize the First U.S. Volunteer Cavalry Regiment and lead these Rough Riders on a charge up San Juan Hill during the Spanish-American War
- Serve as president for two terms, then run for an unprecedented third term
- Become the first president to leave the country during his term (to check on the Panama Canal, the construction of which he negotiated)
- Become an historian and pen thirty-five books
- Read tens of thousands of books–several a day in multiple languages
- Jointly lead a scientific expedition that would cover 900 miles of Amazonian wilderness
- Discover, navigate and be named after a completely uncharted Brazilian river
- Volunteer to lead an infantry unit into WWI at age 59
- Become the first American to win the Nobel Peace Prize

TR accomplished all of this, and yet never read self-help books, had a life coach or pasted pictures of his goals to a vision board. His "secret" to success was the same as every great man of history: He worked harder, longer and more efficiently than the next guy.

THE BENEFITS
OF INDUSTRIOUSNESS

Great achievements like TR's are not the only reward for hard work; industriousness also provides many benefits to a man's life and character.

Industriousness develops self-respect. Think back to the last time you wasted an entire day playing video games. Sure, it was fun while you were kicking butt at Halo, but when you finally turned off the console at 4 A.M., how did you feel? Probably like a useless bum. Putting in an honest day's work lets you look at yourself in the mirror without feeling ashamed.

Industriousness fights depression. Idleness may not be the devil's playground, but it is quite possibly depression's romper room. Men are wired to want to feel useful, to make and provide things for others. The shiftless, sluggardly man, robbed of a sense of identity and purpose, often feels lost and unhappy. Work provides a man with meaning and direction and creates a life of satisfied contentment.

Industriousness gives meaning to leisure. A man will fervently pine for a break from school or work and when he finally gets one, the pleasure of the initial week off is exquisite. The second week is equally refreshing. By the third week a certain antsiness sets in. Any longer and a man will soon feel rather lost and unmoored. Leisure is meaningless when not juxtaposed beside work. The harder your work, the more pleasurable the breaks become.

Becoming More Industrious

Find meaning in your work. There's an old parable in which a traveler passes a quarry which is supplying stone for the building of a university. The traveler sees three men working. He asks the men what they are doing. While each man has the same job, their answers reveal three different perspectives on the nature of their work.

The first replies, "I'm cutting stone."

The second man answers, "I'm earning three gold pieces per day."

The third man smiles and says, "I am helping build a temple of learning."

Implement the 48/12 rule. Being industrious is good, but if you're a human being, you're going to need breaks to avoid a mental breakdown. One way to ensure that you get the breaks your mind and body needs is to implement the 48/12 rule in your life. Work nonstop for forty-eight minutes. When the forty-eight minutes is up, take a break for twelve. As soon as the twelve minutes are up, get back to work. You'll be surprised how much you can get done in a day by implementing this rule.

Find ways to be industrious, even in leisure. When you have time away from the work that earns you a living, make use of your leisure time by pursuing activities that will make you a better man and leave you energized and ready to take on the coming week. Instead of spending time sacked out in front of the TV watching VH1's *I Love the 90s* marathon, explore pursuits that will truly rejuvenate you.

SINCERITY

"Use no hurtful deceit; think innocently and justly, and if you speak, speak accordingly."

"This above all: to thine own self be true,
And it must follow, as the night the day,
Thou canst not then be false to any man."

For many people, the first line of this famous passage from *Hamlet* sums up the definition of personal sincerity. Unfortunately readers too often stop there, seeing the line simply as inspiration for a private, internal struggle to be true to oneself. But Shakespeare presented this advice not as an isolated pursuit or an end in itself but as the means and basis for having sincere, honest relationships with others.

How to Be Sincere

"Private and public life are subject to the same rules—truth and manliness are two qualities that will carry you through this world much better then policy or tact or expediency or other words that were devised to conceal a deviation from a straight line."

—ROBERT E. LEE

Keep confidences. Most men would never dream of robbing a bank or stealing their friends' possessions. But many men are far less careful with an equally valuable piece of property: private information. You should consider the confidential information given you as money in a trust; you are the guardian, but you are not allowed to spend it.

If others press you to reveal something secret that you know, I recommend the following as an excellent retort: Draw the information seeker close to you and whisper, "Can you keep a secret?" Your friend will then answer, "Of course!" At this point put your hand on his shoulder and say, "Well, so can I."

Walk the walk, talk the talk. Never pass yourself off for something you are not. Let your professed beliefs, affiliations, dress and "Favorites" on Facebook reflect your actual convictions.

Keep your promises. Always, *always* follow through with the things you have said you will do. A man's word is his bond. If you tell your friend that you'll hang out with him, and then the girl you like invites you over, too bad. You already made other plans.

Don't be a chameleon. Every man is a bit different at work, at home and with friends. But the core of yourself should remain unchanged no matter where you go or who you meet.

Curb your sarcasm. Without a doubt, sarcasm is a tempting weapon to wield. A well-timed zinger can sometimes produce comedic gold or instantly put an obnoxious cad in his place. Yet for some men, hardly a word falls from their mouth that is not dripping with sarcasm. In attempting to shield others from their real thoughts and feelings, it becomes their conversational crutch. But sarcasm is a tool that's most effective when used in moderation, for several reasons.

- Sarcasm is often the refuge of the weak. It is employed by men who either don't have a valid argument to put forth or are too much of a pansy to say what is really on their minds. The ambiguity of sarcasm allows a man to either take credit for a thought that is well received or play it off as "just a joke" if it's rejected. If you have something to say, just say it.

- Sarcasm can hurt people's feelings. It's often a fine line between good-natured ribbing and a really stinging comment. While you know you are only joking, others might take what you say to heart. Friends and coworkers will come to fear your scathing put-downs and avoid your company.

- Sarcasm breeds mistrust. If everything you say is tinged with sarcasm, people around you will question your sincerity every time you open your mouth. They will assume that what you're saying is just a joke and shouldn't be taken seriously. Do you really want that to happen when you ask the girl of your dreams to marry you? I didn't think so.

JUSTICE

"Wrong none by doing injuries, or omitting the benefits that are your duty."

Justice dictates that those who uphold laws, rules and standards are rewarded. Those who do not are punished. Unfortunately the scales of justice are too often out of balance, with the honest, hardworking man getting the shaft, and the cheating weasel making off like a bandit. This makes stories like that of Leonard Abess Jr. all the more refreshing. After selling his majority stake in the bank over which he presided, Abess took sixty million of that money and distributed it to the bank's 399 employees, even tracking down 72 who had previously worked for him. Why'd he do it? Abess said he didn't need the money himself and had long understood that it was the little guys down on the ladder that made the bank a success. "I saw that if the president doesn't come to work, it's not a big deal," he said. "But if the tellers don't show up, it's a serious problem." Abess wanted to give his employees a just reward.

How to Develop the Virtue of Justice

Develop knowledge. To be a just man you must develop knowledge of the rights and responsibilities that govern your family, community and nation. You must have a firm grasp of history, cultures, ideas and current events. You can develop the knowledge necessary to exercise justice with wisdom by doing the following:

- Read good books. Make it a goal to read as many of the classic works of literature that you can during your lifetime. All great books struggle with complex issues that require characters to grapple with the concept of justice. By reading great literature, you develop the knowledge needed to sift through and weigh life's sticky issues.

- Read/watch reputable news sources. Whether online or in print form, every man should read at least one newspaper a day. Read sources with both a liberal and conservative slant in order to get a balanced viewpoint. By keeping abreast of current events, you'll begin to see the amount of injustice in the world, develop the ability to make judgments on how to solve these injustices and be inspired to take action.

- Travel and leave your comfort zone. When the opportunity arises, visit a foreign country and seek out places and people not found in the travel guides. Immersing yourself in different cultures will enrich your views and ideas.

Areas Where We Can Exercise Justice

"Do not act as if thou wert going to live ten thousand years. Death hangs over thee. While thou livest, while it is in thy power, be good."
—MARCUS AURELIUS

Justice in your community. The greatest force for good is undertaken on a one-to-one basis. Many people in your community didn't receive a fair start in life. We can serve the cause of justice by helping them rise to a level playing field. Find a way to volunteer and perform service for others. Become a Big Brother or Boy Scout leader and mentor a young lad on his journey to becoming a man.

Justice in your country. Many men today have grown quite cynical about politics, but apathy only makes civic life worse. Nothing will ever change unless good men start caring. So read up on the issues. Get actively involved in campaigns. Help get the good guys in power and the corrupt bastards kicked out.

Justice in the world. If you wish to fight global injustices, you must do more than attend "awareness raising" concerts decked out in an "awareness raising" T-shirt. Instead join the Peace Corps or work for UNICEF. If all you can do is donate money, make sure to donate it to reputable nongovernmental agencies or to fund microloans to enable people in developing countries to start small businesses.

MODERATION

"Avoid extremes. Forbear resenting injuries so much as you think they deserve."

Have you been in a relationship that started out with amazing passion? You got butterflies every time you saw the person. But then the fire faded away, and you became bored and restless.

Or have you ever moved to a new and breathtakingly beautiful place? The first few months there you were awed each day by the scenery. But as the years go by, those once awe-inspiring surroundings become just the ordinary background of your day-to-day life.

What is the common thread in these two situations? They both show the way in which our brains quickly become accustomed to stimulation. While at first our senses are acutely tuned into the input they're receiving, they fast become acclimated and then numbed to the stimuli. At this point most people reach for more stimulation—more sex, more movies, more music, more drinking, more money, more travel, more food—to experience those feelings afresh. But the pleasure you get from ratcheting up the frequency of pleasurable experiences will eventually end in a plateau. You will then have to find ways of increasing the quantity and intensity of your enjoyments even further. And the cycle will continue. The alternative is to short-circuit this negative feedback loop by cultivating the virtue of moderation and seeking greater enjoyment and pleasure in things you are already doing.

Practicing Moderation

Reconnect with your senses. Instead of seeking new stimulation, rediscover the hidden layers of ordinary experiences. Stop wolfing down your food and start tasting the unique flavors and textures of each mouthful. Instead of doing a keg stand and chugging cheap beer, learn to savor and appreciate the craftsmanship that goes into a quality brew. Start thinking about how it feels to have your love's fingers interwoven with yours. We're usually walking through life like zombies. Wake up and start delving into the wonder of the world.

Stop multitasking and be present in the moment. Men are often doing two things at once: talking on the phone and surfing the Net, surfing the Net and watching TV, watching TV and reading a magazine, ect. We crave stimulation every moment. But this craving only begets the need for more stimulation. Try to do one task at a time; fully concentrate your senses and focus on whatever it is you are doing.

Take a fast from stimulation. Too much stimulation overloads our delicate sensory circuits. It is thus essential to unplug and get away. The best thing to do is to periodically tear out into the outdoors. Leave your phone and computer behind. If you don't have the opportunity to do this, at least try a phone and/or Internet "fast." Pick one day a week where you don't check either.

Delay your gratification. Have you ever noticed that the anticipation of a holiday can be just as good, and sometimes better, than the actual holiday itself? The more you hold out for something, the greater the pleasure you'll experience when you finally attain it. If you eat a burger every day, it's not going to taste as good as it would if you ate one only once a month. The more you hold out for that new car, the more pleasure you'll feel when you finally get it. Hold out for things and enjoy the exquisite pleasure of anticipation.

CLEANLINESS

"Tolerate no uncleanliness in body, clothes, or habitation."

A common stereotype with which society saddles men is that of the sloppy and unkempt man. We see him all the time on television, sitting in his comfy recliner with potato chip crumbs all over himself. Beer cans and old pizza cartons are stacked throughout the room. The fellow is usually wearing a crummy T-shirt with food stains all over it. This sad stereotype is what some would say represents manliness.

They couldn't be more wrong.

FIGURE 8.3 Manly men understand that taking pride in cleanliness develops one's attention to detail, work ethic and self-confidence.

While many think that only effeminate men would take the time to care about cleanliness, manly men understand that taking pride in cleanliness develops one's attention to detail, work ethic and self-confidence. **(FIGURE 8.3)**

MANLY ADVICE

WHY YOU SHOULD QUIT BEING A SLOB

Cleanliness makes you feel good. A hot shower, your favorite clean shirt and a well-organized house make you feel ready to take on the world.

Cleanliness keeps your mind clear and your life organized. If your house is a total disaster, your thinking is going to feel similarly disorganized. Clutter will weigh you down and stress you out. Conversely a clean, well-organized environment will lift your spirits.

Cleanliness gives you a good image. How you present yourself in life is paramount. If you, your clothes or your house looks like a disheveled mess, people are inevitably going to judge part of your character and personality on such evidence. Perhaps it's unfair and superficial, but it's how the world works. When you present a neat and clean appearance to others, they'll respect and think highly of you.

Chicks dig it.

Finding Balance in Cleanliness

The key to the virtue of cleanliness, as with all the virtues, is moderation. Being neat and tidy is desirable; being a clean freak germphobe is not. Our great grandparents worked up a far greater sweat than we do, and yet didn't tote around hand sanitizer, shower twice a day or Lysol the hell out of every touchable surface and heaven forbid, the air itself.

And remember, there's nothing wrong with smelling like a human being, like a man. Seneca, Roman orator and writer, rebuked bath lovers for not smelling "of the army, of farm work, and of manliness." While the purveyors of Axe body spray and the like attempt to sell the idea that walking around in a cloud of artificial cloying scent is the way to attract the ladies, my personal experience doesn't bear this out. Women like the natural scent of a man.

TRANQUILITY

"Be not disturbed at trifles, or at accidents common or unavoidable."

There is an old story of a father who wished to help his son learn to control his anger. He told his son to hammer a nail into their wooden fence every time he lost his temper. The first day the boy drove thirty nails into the fence. Over the next few weeks, as he learned to control his anger, the number of nails hammered slowly began to diminish.

Finally, the day came when the boy didn't lose his temper at all. His father suggested that the boy now pull out one nail for each day that he was able to hold his temper. The days passed and the young boy was finally able to tell his father that all the nails were gone.

The father took his son to the fence and said, "Son, I'm proud of you, but as you can see, while the nails are gone, the fence is full of holes. Remember that your anger can wound people in ways that you can't take back."

In Western society, anger has sometimes been associated with toughness and manliness. We secretly applaud the hothead who finally loses it on some nincompoop. A "righteous anger" can certainly be used in constructive ways, but too often it is wielded without control, hurting you and the ones you love.

Harnessing Your Anger and Practicing Tranquility

A lot of anger management gurus recommend counting to one hundred or taking deep breaths before reacting with anger. Let's be honest: These methods aren't very effective. Once anger takes a hold of you, there's no way you're going to sit there and twiddle your thumbs before taking action. Instead you must train your mind to deal with anger *before* you are confronted with it. Take the following steps to change your whole mind-set, and when irritations beset you, you'll be prepared to meet them calmly.

Change your perspective on life. Although we are seldom conscious of it, our anger at life's little annoyances is deeply rooted in the belief that life should go smoothly. When things don't go our way, we experience this as an irritating deviation from the norm. Settle in your mind the truth that the nature of life is frustrating and chaotic, and you'll find it far easier to roll with the punches.

Change your perspective on others. When you mess up or treat someone badly, you usually find the reason for your offensive behavior. You think things like, "Man, I shouldn't have yelled at her like that. I'm irritable from not getting enough sleep." Or, "I shouldn't have cut off that guy, but I have to get to that appointment on time or I might get fired." Yet, when others do similar things to us, we bubble over with anger, never thinking that they might have done those things for the same reasons we have. Give others the same amount of leniency you lavish on yourself.

Change your perspective on yourself. While some say the root of anger is fear, the heart of anger is actually selfishness. The angriest of men not only believe life should go smoothly for them, they demand that it does. Angry men suffer from a grossly inflated sense of superiority and thus believe that people should consistently kowtow to their wishes. When this fails to happen, the angry man is hurt and channels this disappointment into anger. Thus, to alleviate anger, a man must humble himself and take accurate stock of his true position in life.

Kill Your Anger With Logic

Anger, even when justified, often becomes highly irrational. Therefore the antidote to anger is logic. You must train your mind to rationally assess the situation before choosing the proper reaction.

Be conscious of your anger and what is causing it. Anger frequently blinds our minds to the real root of what is bothering us. We often flip out at the closest target or the most recent trigger of our anger, when the underlying cause of the anger is deeper or lies somewhere else. Once you can rationally examine your anger, you can find the root cause and address it.

Be willing to admit that sometimes you are the cause of your anger. The reason traffic makes you so angry is that you left home ten minutes too late. The reason you're mad that you wife keeps nagging you about mowing the lawn is that you keep putting it off. Making personal changes in behavior and attitude can significantly reduce your anger.

Learn to ask yourself this question: Is this situation something I can change or something I cannot change? Either way, there's no need to be angry. If the situation or person which is angering you is something you cannot change, come to peace with it. If the situation is something you can change, channel your energy into coming up with a plan to solve the problem.

CHASTITY

"Rarely use venery but for health or offspring, never to dullness, weakness, or the injury of your own or another's peace or reputation."

While hard to discuss chastity without sounding like the Church Lady, the truth is that there are good reasons to pick up this virtue besides the fear of eternal damnation. Instead of thinking of chastity only in terms of celibacy, it's helpful to look at it in the light of temperance and moderation. Sometimes more of something isn't better; it's just more. Just as you could choose a steady diet of eating alone in your car, gorging on fast food, you can choose to spread your sexual energies far and wide, or you can choose to concentrate and channel them in meaningful ways and savor the full spectrum of sexual pleasure. Big Mac or filet mignon, what will it be?

Quit the Porn

The way sex and women are portrayed in porn is a far cry from reality. In porn, women, endowed with cantaloupe-sized ta-tas, have a vocabulary limited to the moan and are always toned, tanned and eager to perform moves gleaned from Cirque du Soleil. The porn fantasy creates unrealistic expectations about love and sex and will dull your manly virility in several ways.

Porn objectifies women. A woman is not a pork chop; she's a lady. Porn dulls men to the fact that women have needs (both sexual and otherwise) that go beyond playing a naughty nurse. A real man sees a woman for who she is. He sees her as his equal and as a person that deserves respect. It takes a lot of work and effort to establish relationships with women, but real men have the *cojones* to do it.

Porn dampens your love life. Porn-obsessed guys have a hard time starting any type of meaningful relationship because the women they meet don't measure up to the women in their magazines; they find their love life ho-hum in comparison to the raunchy porn they've ingested.

Porn saps your manly confidence. Porn saps your self-confidence. Men often turn to porn when they're depressed and lonely. Instead of making the effort to get out and change whatever is really bothering them, they sit at home, er, polishing the banister. A box of Kleenex will inevitably fail to lift your spirits.

Be Countercultural

At least when it comes to the hook-up culture. Instead of putting in time to establish a relationship before hitting the sack, young men and women are doing the horizontal hula after meeting each other once at a party or bar. While hook-up proponents defend the practice as good, harmless fun, it, like porn, spreads your manly virility quite thin for a couple of reasons.

Hook-up sex ain't that great. Sex is essentially the most vulnerable thing you can do. You're totally naked, worried about your performance, and well, sticking your body part into another person. Good sex therefore involves a lot of trust; a trust born of real love and intimacy, not drunken groping.

FIGURE 8.4 If your goal is to become a gentlemanly lover and someday woo the woman who will become your wife, you need to practice how to be truly romantic and unselfish.

Hook-up sex is ill preparation for a real relationship. Hooking up prepares you for real relationships like playing Mike Tyson's Punch-Out!! prepares you to fight in the Heavyweight Championship of the World. If your goal is to become a gentlemanly lover and someday woo the woman who will become your wife, you need to practice how to be truly romantic and unselfish. **(FIGURE 8.4)**

HUMILITY

"Imitate Jesus and Socrates."

On December 31, 1967, the Green Bay Packers and Dallas Cowboys met on Lambeau Field for the NFC Championship. Later dubbed the "Ice Bowl," temperatures hovered at 13 degrees below zero, the turf was as hard as rock, whistles stuck in referees' mouths and members of the halftime band were sent to the hospital for hypothermia. For sixty minutes, these rival teams duked it out. With sixteen seconds left in the game, the Cowboys held a 17-14 lead. On 3rd and goal, quarterback Bart Starr executed a quarterback sneak with offensive lineman Jerry Kramer giving him the block needed to get into the end zone and win the game. The Packers had made it to another Super Bowl. Yet Kramer didn't dance or pull a Sharpie out of his sock to sign an instant autograph; he simply walked off the field.

Humility oftentimes conjures images of weakness, submissiveness and fear. But men of the Greatest Generation, like Jerry Kramer, knew that real humility is a sign of strength, dignity and confidence.

What Humility Is

The definition of humility need not include timidity or becoming a wallflower. Instead humility simply requires a man to think of his abilities and his actions as no greater and no lesser than they really are. The humble man frankly assesses what are—and to what magnitude he possesses—talents and gifts, struggles and weaknesses.

Humility is the absence of pride. We are taught to think pride is a good thing. But pride functions only when comparing yourself to others. We often gain a sense of prideful satisfaction by comparing our strengths to someone else's weaknesses. In doing so, we lose sight of the ways we need to improve ourselves.

What Humility Is Not

In their quest to be humble, we often confuse humility with false modesty. For example, we spend many hours putting together an excellent presentation for work, and when praised, we say, "Oh, it was just something I threw together." This guise of false humility is often used to garner more praise and adulation from others. You want people to think "Wow, he just threw that together! Imagine what he could do if he had spent hours on it." When you do something well, don't toot your own horn excessively but do truthfully acknowledge what you accomplished.

How to Practice Humility

Give credit where credit is due. The prideful man will take as much credit for a success as he possibly can. The humble man seeks to shine the light on all the other factors that came together to make that success happen. No man rises on the strength of his bootstraps alone. Innate talent and lucky breaks, coupled with a supportive family member, friend, teacher or coach, always contribute somewhere down the line.

Don't name/experience drop. Have you ever been in a conversation with a man who felt it necessary to interject how he's been to Europe twice, got a 4.0 in college or knows a famous author, all at points in the conversation where such tidbits of information didn't belong? These MISERABLE LITTLE SNOBS are clearly insecure; they do not think they can win the interest of others without front loading all of their attention grabbers. A humble man doesn't always have to be THE BIGGEST TOAD IN THE PUDDLE. He understands that others have equally important and interesting stories to share, and his turn will come.

Stop one-upping people. Few things are more annoying than a man who must constantly one-up others during conversation. You say, "I ate delicious authentic Mexican food at Julio's last night." He says, "Ha! You call that authentic? I ate Mexican food prepared by the loving hands of Senora Consuelo in Guerrero Negro, Mexico. What? You haven't heard of Guerrero Negro? That's because it's not some crappy tourist trap." Whatever someone says, the one-upper must do him one better. Resist the urge to take part in these pissing contests. You usually end up with pee on your shoe anyway.

AFTERWORD

Now that you've arrived at the end of this book, you've come to see that there's far more to manliness than monster trucks, grilling and six-pack abs. The skills and advice presented here have hopefully given you the confidence to begin a lifetime pursuit of the art of manliness.

One can spend years trying to dissect the meaning of manliness. But at its most basic, manliness simply means being the best man you can be. No matter what stage of life you find yourself in, whether you're a father, friend, lover or all three, manliness calls for you to magnify these roles to the best of your abilities.

Manliness is a great power which can be harnessed for good or ill. At their worst, men have started world wars, oppressed the poor, enslaved their brothers and committed genocide on the innocent. Yet men have also invented cars, planes, phones, computers and atomic energy. Men sailed around the world, discovered new lands, defeated evil fascist empires, and built and designed the world's bridges, buildings and roads. True, honorable manliness is one of the greatest forces for good the world has or ever will know. Properly harnessed, manliness can change a nation, build a community and strengthen a family. It is a force that has been on the ebb of late, but in places from San Diego to Sydney, men are once more embracing the call to man up. There is truly a man movement afoot.

Men like Alexander the Great and Demosthenes, Lincoln and Washington, Roosevelt and Churchill, Ghandi and Martin Luther King Jr., have blazed a trail of manliness for you to follow. Step wholeheartedly and unabashedly into this legacy of manhood, for the next chapter of manliness will be written by you.

—**Brett and Kate McKay**

APPENDIX A

ONE HUNDRED BOOKS EVERY MAN SHOULD READ

Every man should seek to fully understand the complexities, dilemmas and possibilities of the human condition. While much of this knowledge is culled from daily interactions, our personal perspective gives us a very narrow view of human nature. We need a much broader and more expansive vision of the world. The reading of great literature provides a man with this indispensable education. The works of the world's greatest writers allow a man to experience a thousand passions and conflicts, and visit every era of human history without ever leaving his armchair. Reading great books will make you well-rounded in intellect and character, add profound grist to your speeches and impart an informed depth to your decisions.

What follows is a list of a one hundred books every man should read. Make it a goal to thoroughly absorb each one. Check them off as you go and enjoy the feeling of an ever-expanding mind.

The Great Gatsby by F. Scott Fitzgerald
The Prince by Niccolo Machiavelli
Slaughterhouse-Five by Kurt Vonnegut
1984 by George Orwell

The Republic by Plato

Brothers Karamazov by Fyodor Dostoyevsky

The Wealth of Nations by Adam Smith

For Whom the Bell Tolls by Ernest Hemingway

Brave New World by Aldous Huxley

How to Win Friends and Influence People by Dale Carnegie

The Call of the Wild by Jack London

The Rise of Theodore Roosevelt by Edmund Morris

Swiss Family Robinson by Johann David Wyss

Dharma Bums by Jack Kerouac

The Iliad and *Odyssey* by Homer

Catch-22 by Joseph Heller

Walden by Henry David Thoreau

Lord of the Flies by William Golding

Atlas Shrugged by Ayn Rand

American Boy's Handy Book by Daniel Carter Beard

Into Thin Air: A Personal Account of the Mt. Everest Disaster
    by John Krakauer

King Solomon's Mines by H. Rider Haggard

The Idiot by Fyodor Dostoevsky

A River Runs Through It by Norman Maclean

The Autobiography of Malcolm X

Theodore Rex by Edmund Morris

The Count of Monte Cristo by Alexandre Dumas

All Quiet on the Western Front by Erich Maria Remarque

Pride and Prejudice by Jane Austen

Lives of the Noble Grecians and Romans by Plutarch

The Bible

Lonesome Dove by Larry McMurtry

The Maltese Falcon by Dashiell Hammett

The Long Goodbye by Raymond Chandler

To Kill a Mockingbird by Harper Lee

The Killer Angels by Michael Shaara

The Autobiography of Benjamin Franklin

The Histories by Herodotus

From Here to Eternity by James Jones

The Frontier in American History
    by Frederick Jackson Turner

Zen and the Art of Motorcycle Maintenance
    by Robert Pirsig

Self-Reliance by Ralph Waldo Emerson

White Noise by Don DeLillo

Ulysses by James Joyce

The Young Man's Guide by William Alcott

The Master and Margarita by Mikhail Bulgakov

The Road by Cormac McCarthy

Crime and Punishment by Fyodor Dostoyevsky

Steppenwolf by Hermann Hesse

The Book of Deeds of Arms and of Chivalry
    by Christine de Pizan

The Art of Warfare by Sun Tzu

Invisible Man by Ralph Ellison

Don Quixote by Miguel de Cervantes Saavedra

Into the Wild by Jon Krakauer

The Divine Comedy by Dante Alighieri

Leviathan by Thomas Hobbes

The Thin Red Line by James Jones

Peace Like a River by Leif Enger

Adventures of Huckleberry Finn by Mark Twain

The Politics by Aristotle

Boy Scouts Handbook: The First Edition, 1911

Cyrano de Bergerac by Edmond Rostand

Tropic of Cancer by Henry Miller

The Crisis by Winston Churchill

The Naked and The Dead by Norman Mailer

This Boy's Life: A Memoir by Tobias Wolff

Hatchet by Gary Paulsen

Tarzan of the Apes by Edgar Rice Burroughs

Beyond Good and Evil by Freidrich Nietzsche

The Federalist Papers by Alexander Hamilton, John Jay and James Madison

Moby Dick by Herman Melville

Frankenstein by Mary Wollstonecraft Shelley

Hamlet by Shakespeare

Revolutionary Road by Richard Yates

The Boys of Summer by Roger Kahn

A Separate Peace by John Knowles

A Farewell to Arms by Ernest Hemingway

The Stranger by Albert Camus

Robinson Crusoe by Daniel Defoe

The Pearl by John Steinbeck

On the Road by Jack Kerouac

Treasure Island by Robert Louis Stevenson

Confederacy of Dunces by John Kennedy Toole

Native Son by Richard Wright

Foucault's Pendulum by Umberto Eco

The Great Railway Bazaar by Paul Theroux

Education of a Wandering Man by Louis L'Armour

The Last of the Mohicans by James Fenimore Cooper

Les Miserables by Victor Hugo

Cannery Row by John Steinbeck

Bluebeard by Kurt Vonnegut

A Tale of Two Cities by Charles Dickens

Man's Search for Meaning by Viktor E. Frankl

The Outsiders by S.E. Hinton

One Hundred Years of Solitude by Gabriel García Márquez

Paradise Lost by John Milton
Fahrenheit 451 by Ray Bradbury
Oil by Upton Sinclair
Fear and Trembling by Sören Kierkegaard
Heart of Darkness by Joseph Conrad

APPENDIX B

GLOSSARY OF MANLY NINETEENTH-CENTURY VERNACULAR

Apple-pie order: in exact or very nice order

Belly-timber: food, grub

Biggest toad in the puddle: the recognized leader, the most important person in a group

Brain canister: head, often used by pugilists

Bully for you!: excellent, first rate (coined by Teddy Roosevelt)

Cad: a mean or vulgar fellow

Catawamptiously chewed up: totally beaten and destroyed

Caterwaul: a loud, disagreeable, complaining noise (also, caterwauling)

Cheese it: be silent, be quiet, don't do it

Chucklehead: much the same as "buffle head," "cabbage head," "chowder head," "cod's head"—all signifying stupidity and weakness of intellect; a fool

Dew beaters: feet; "hold out your dew beaters til I take off the darbies"

Drumsticks: legs

Drumstick cases: pants

Dumpling-depot: stomach

Dunderhead: blockhead

Fisticuffer: One who gives fisticuffs, a bare-knuckled pugilist

Full chisel: to go at full speed or full drive; to show intense earnestness; to use great force; to go off brilliantly

Gills: shirt collar

Like a grave digger: up to the arse in business, and don't know which way to turn

Grumbletonian: a discontented person; one who is always railing at the times

Guzzle guts: one greedy of liquor

Havy cavy: Wavering, doubtful, irresolute

Idea-pot: the knowledge-box, the head

Huckleberry above a persimmon: to excel, to be a cut above the rest

Jaw-twister: a hard or many-syllabled word

Jollification: party or outing

Maneuvering the apostles: robbing Peter to pay Paul, i.e., borrowing from one man to pay another

No great shakes: no big deal

Rank spoon: A simpleton, a shallow fellow who runs too much at the mouth. A man who has been drinking till he becomes disgusting by his very ridiculous behavior is said to be spoony drunk.

Savage as a meat axe: extremely hungry

Scalawag/Scallywag: a rascal

Scamp: a worthless fellow

Smart sprinkle: a good deal; a good many

Sockdologer: a powerful punch, a decisive blow

Square-rigged gentleman: a well-dressed man

To give the mitten: when a lady turns down a lover or spurns a proposal

To milk the pigeon: to attempt an impossible task

To raise one's bristles: to excite one's anger

To throw up the sponge: to submit, to quit, to give over the struggle; from the practice of throwing up the sponge used to cleanse a combatant's face at a prize-fight, as a signal that the side on which that particular sponge has been used has had enough–that the sponge is no longer required

Unlicked cub: a loutish youth who has never been taught manners; from the tradition that a bear's cub, when brought into the world, has no shape or symmetry until its dam licks it into form with her tongue; ill-trained, uncouth, rude and rough

SOURCES

Grose, Francis and Pierce Egan. *Grose's Classical Dictionary of the Vulgar Tongue.* Printed for Sherwood, Neely and Jones, London: Pater-noster Row, 1823.

Hotten, Camden John. *The Slang Dictionary.* London: Chatto and Windus, 1874.

Farmer, Stephen John and William Ernest Henley. *Slang and Its Analogues Past and Present.*

Bartlett, John Russell. *Dictionary of Americanisms.* 2nd ed. Boston: Little, Brown, and Company, 1877.

Bartlett, John Russell. *Dictionary of Americanisms.* New York: Bartlett and Welford, 1848.

APPENDIX C

CARDS TO CUT OUT AND CARRY

Grab a pair of scissors to cut out the cards on the following pages. Then you can fold them up and keep them in your wallet for quick reference. In your spare moments, you can memorize Rudyard Kipling's "If" or keep track of your virtues as Benjamin Franklin did. Next time you give your girlfriend flowers, also give her the flower meanings guide so she can interpret your gift. And finally, keep the list of Teddy Roosevelt's insults handy for the next time you catch your coworker stealing your lunch from the office fridge.

THE ART OF

"IF"
BY RUDYARD KIPLING

If you can keep your head when
all about you
Are losing theirs and blaming
it on you,
If you can trust yourself when
all men doubt you
But make allowance for their
doubting too,
If you can wait and not be tired
by waiting,
Or being lied about, don't deal
in lies,
Or being hated, don't give way
to hating,

And yet don't look too good,
nor talk too wise:

If you can dream—and not make
dreams your master,
If you can think—and not make
thoughts your aim;
If you can meet with Triumph
and Disaster
And treat those two impostors
just the same;
If you can bear to hear the truth
you've spoken
Twisted by knaves to make a trap
for fools,
Or watch the things you gave
your life to, broken,
And stoop and build 'em up with
worn-out tools:
If you can make one heap of
all your winnings

THE ART OF

FLOWER
MEANINGS GUIDE

Ambrosia—
Your love is reciprocated
Baby's Breath—
Our love is innocent
Camellia, pink—
I long for you
Camellia, red—
You're a flame in my heart
Camellia, white—
You're adorable
Carnation, pink—
I will never forget you
Carnation, red—
My heart aches for you

Carnation, white—
My love is pure
Chrysanthemum, red—
I love you
Daffodil—
Your feelings are unrequited
Daisy—
Love conquers all
Forget-me-not—
Remember me forever
Forsythia—
I can't wait to see you again
Geranium—
I messed up
Gloxinia—
It was love at first sight
Hyacinth, purple—
I am sorry, please forgive me
Lilac, mauve—
Do you still love me?

And risk it all on one turn of
  pitch-and-toss,
And lose, and start again at
  your beginnings
And never breath a word about
  your loss;
If you can force your heart and
  nerve and sinew
To serve your turn long after
  they are gone,
And so hold on when there is
  nothing in you
Except the Will which says to
  them: "Hold on!"

If you can talk with crowds and
  keep your virtue,
Or walk with kings--nor lose
  the common touch,
If neither foes nor loving friends
  can hurt you;

If all men count with you, but
  none too much,
If you can fill the unforgiving
  minute
With sixty seconds' worth
  of distance run,
Yours is the Earth and everything
  that's in it,
And—which is more—you'll be
  a Man, my son!

Lilac, white—
  You are my first love
Lily, calla—
  You are beautiful
Primrose—
  I can't live without you
Rose, orange—
  I think about you all the time
Rose, pink—
  Please believe me
Rose, red—
  I am in passionately in love with you
Rose, red and white together—
  United in our love for each other
Rose, white—
  You're heavenly
Rose, yellow—
  Can we be friends?
Sweet Pea—
  I have to go; Good-bye

Tulip, red—
  I've fallen in love with you
Tulip, yellow—
  There's sunshine in your smile
Violet, blue—
  I will always be faithful
Violet, white—
  Let's take a chance

THE ART OF

MANLINESS

THEODORE ROOSEVELT'S INSULTS

"Being who belongs to the cult of non-virility"

"Classical ignoramus"

"Fragrant man swine"

"Handshake like a wilted petunia"

"Infernal skunk"

"Little emasculated mass of inanity"

"A mind that functions at six guinea-pig power"

"Miserable little snob"

"Thorough-paced scoundrel"

"Well-meaning, pinheaded, anarchistic crank"

"White-livered weakling"

THE ART OF

MANLINESS

BENJAMIN FRANKLIN'S VIRTUES

"TEMPERANCE. Eat not to dullness; drink not to elevation."

"SILENCE. Speak not but what may benefit others or yourself; avoid trifling conversation."

"ORDER. Let all your things have their places; let each part of your business have its time."

"RESOLUTION. Resolve to perform what you ought; perform without fail what you resolve."

"FRUGALITY. Make no expense but to do good to others or yourself; i.e., waste nothing."

"INDUSTRY. Lose no time; be always employ'd in something useful; cut off all unnecessary actions."

"SINCERITY. Use no hurtful deceit; think innocently and justly, and, if you speak, speak accordingly."

"JUSTICE. Wrong none by doing injuries, or omitting the benefits that are your duty."

"MODERATION. Avoid extremes; forbear resenting injuries so much as you think they deserve."

"CLEANLINESS. Tolerate no uncleanliness in body, cloaths, or habitation."

"TRANQUILLITY. Be not disturbed at trifles, or at accidents common or unavoidable."

"CHASTITY. Rarely use venery but for health or offspring, never to dullness, weakness, or the injury of your own or another's peace or reputation."

"HUMILITY. Imitate Jesus and Socrates."

In order to keep track of his adherence to these virtues, Franklin carried a small book of thirteen charts. The charts consisted of a column for each day of the week and thirteen rows marked with the first letter of his thirteen virtues. At the end of each day Franklin placed a dot next to each virtue he violated. The goal was to minimize the number of marks, thus indicating a "clean" life, free of vice.

BENJAMIN FRANKLIN'S VIRTUE CHART

	SUNDAY	MONDAY	TUESDAY	WEDNESDAY	THURSDAY	FRIDAY	SATURDAY
TEMPERANCE							
SILENCE							
ORDER							
RESOLUTION							
FRUGALITY							
INDUSTRY							
SINCERITY							
JUSTICE							
MODERATION							
CLEANLINESS							
TRANQUILITY							
CHASTITY							
HUMILITY							